FISHING HOT SPOTS
OF THE UPPER FRASER VALLEY

Richard Evan Probert

hancock
house

ISBN 0-88839-307-5
Copyright © 1992 Richard E. Probert

Second Printing 1997

Cataloging in Publication Data
Probert, Richard Evan, 1946-
    Fishing hot spots of the Upper Fraser Valley

    Includes bibliographical references.
    ISBN 0-88839-307-5

    1. Fishing—British Columbia—Fraser River Valley—Guidebooks. 2. Fraser River Valley (B.C.)—Guidebooks. I. Title.
    SH572.B7P76 1992   799.1'09711'37   C92-091317-2

All rights reserved. No part of this publication may be reproduced, stored in a retrieval system or transmitted, in any form or by any means, electronic, mechanical, photocopying, recording, or otherwise, without the prior written permission of Hancock House Publishers.
Printed in Hong Kong—Colorcraft

Cover photo: Marge Dyer
Back cover photo: Don Beaton
Production: Lorna Lake

Published simultaneously in Canada and the United States by

HANCOCK HOUSE PUBLISHERS LTD.
19313 Zero Avenue, Surrey, B.C. V4P 1M7
(604) 538-1114   Fax (604) 538-2262

HANCOCK HOUSE PUBLISHERS
1431 Harrison Avenue, Blaine, WA 98230-5005
(604) 538-1114   Fax (604) 538-2262

"There is a rhythm to an anglers life and a rhythm to his year."

—Nick Lyons
The Seasonable Angler

CONTENTS

	Area Map 1	8
	Area Map 2	10
	Area Map 3	12
	Area Map 4	14
I	**FOR SMALL FRY AND BEGINNERS**	16
	INTRODUCTION	17
1	Deer Lake	20
2	Trout Lake	24
3	Maria Slough	26
4	Hicks Lake	31
5	Johnson's Slough	33
6	Slough Under Agassiz Bridge	34
7	Pump House Slough	36
8	Tranmer's Bar	38
9	Morrow's Bar	40
10	Miami River	42
11	Bouchard's Slough	43
12	Hope River	45
13	Kawkawa Lake	45
14	Silver Lake	45
15	Lake of the Woods	45
II	**FOR THE KNOWLEDGEABLE & EXPERIENCED**	46
16	The Beaver Pond	47
17	Weaver Lake	49
18	Morris Lake	50
19	Harrison River	51
20	Elbow Lake	53
21	Grace Lake	53
22	Francis Lake	53
23	Wolf Lake	53
24	Wood Lake	53
25	Foley Lake	54

26	Tunnels Bar	55
27	Island 22 Park	56
28	Lindeman and Greendrop lakes	57
29	Other Chilliwack Area Bars	58
30	The Vedder-Chilliwack River	59
31	Under Agassiz Bridge on the Rosedale Side	61
32	Chilliwack Lake	62
33	Cultus Lake	62
34	Chehalis Lake	62
35	Jones Lake	62
36	Coqulhala River	62
III	**FOR THE DEDICATED AND SKILLED**	64
37	The Chehalis River	65
38	Harrison Lake	67
39	Slollicum Lake	68
40	Statlu Lake	69
41	Weaver Creek	70
42	Moss Lake	70
43	Lookout Lake	70
44	Campbell Lake	70
45	Wilson Lake	71
46	Flora Lake	71
47	Pierce Lake	71
48	Crescent Lake	71
49	Hanging Lake	71
IV	**GAME FISH AND THEIR HABITS**	72
	The Life Cycle of Pacific Salmonids	73
	Salmonid Migration	74
	Game Fish in the Upper Fraser Valley	77
	Fishing Tips	83
	Tackle Tips for Beginners	84
	Releasing Fish	85
	Solunar Periods/Fishing Licenses/	86
	Fishing Guide	87
	Stocking Data	87
	REFERENCES	88

THE FRASER VALLEY

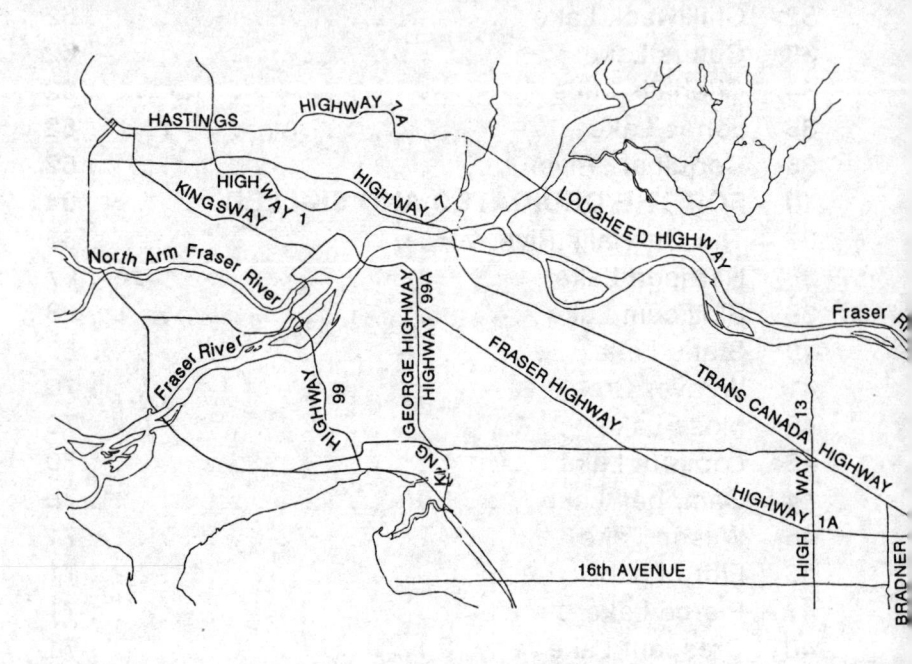

AREA MAP 1

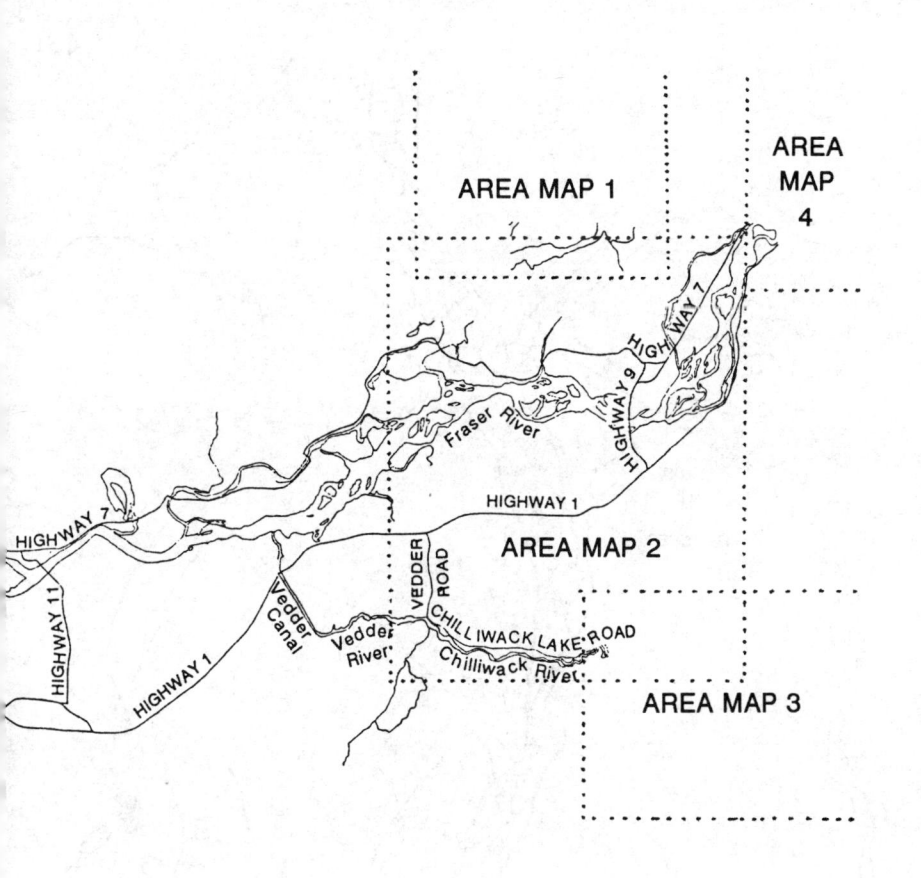

AREA MAP 4

AREA MAP 2

AREA MAP 3

Fraser River
HIGHWAY 9
HIGHWAY 7
HIGHWAY 1
VEDDER ROAD
CHILLIWACK LAKE ROAD
Vedder Canal
Vedder River
Chilliwack River
HIGHWAY 7
HIGHWAY 11
HIGHWAY 1

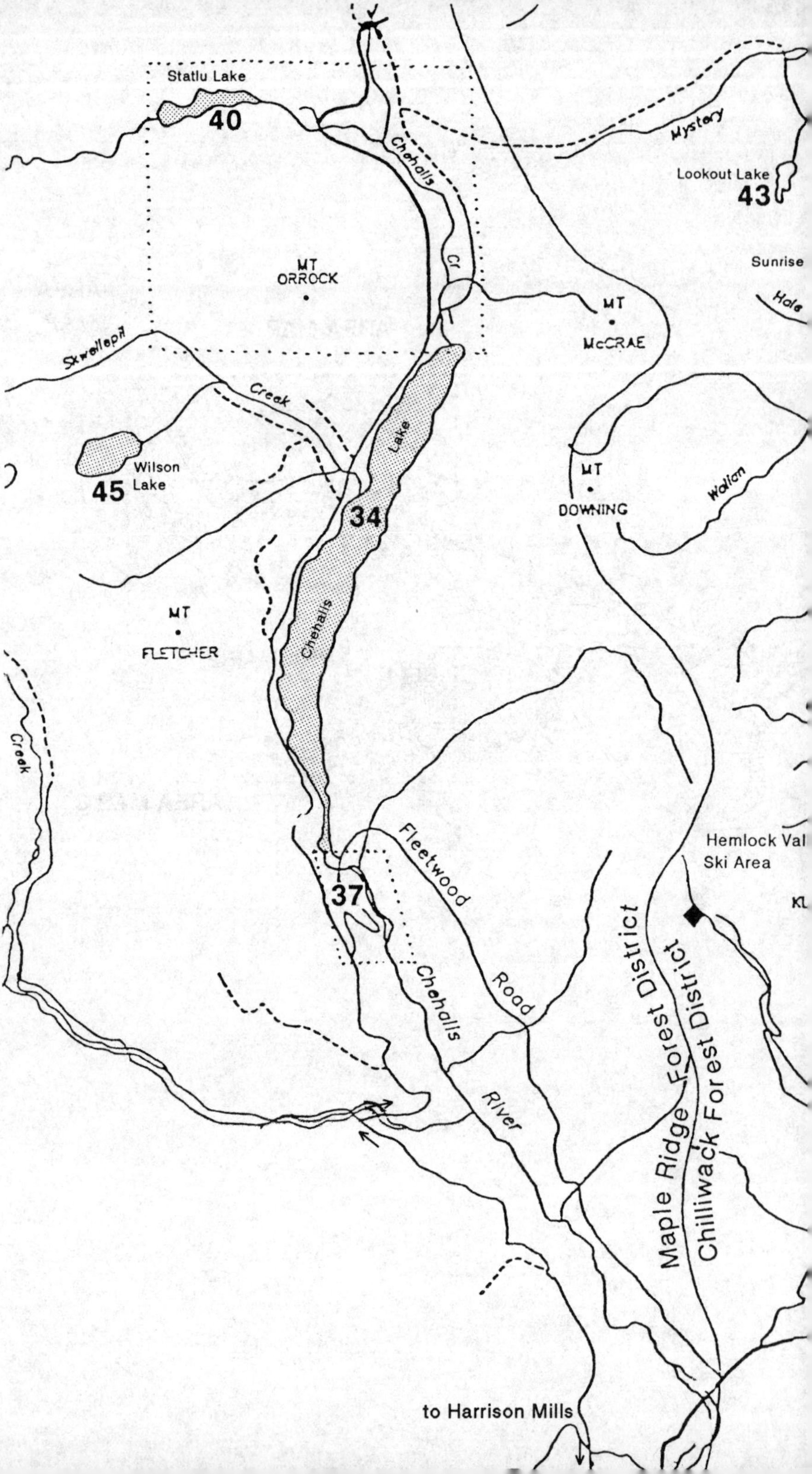

Statlu Lake
40
Chehalis
Cr
Mystery
Lookout Lake
43
Sunrise
Hale
MT
ORROCK
MT
McCRAE
Skwellepil
Creek
Lake
Wilson
Lake
45
34
MT
DOWNING
Wallan
MT
FLETCHER
Chehalis
Creek
Fleetwood
Road
37
Chehalis
River
Hemlock Val
Ski Area
KL
Maple Ridge Forest District
Chilliwack Forest District
to Harrison Mills

AREA MAP 1

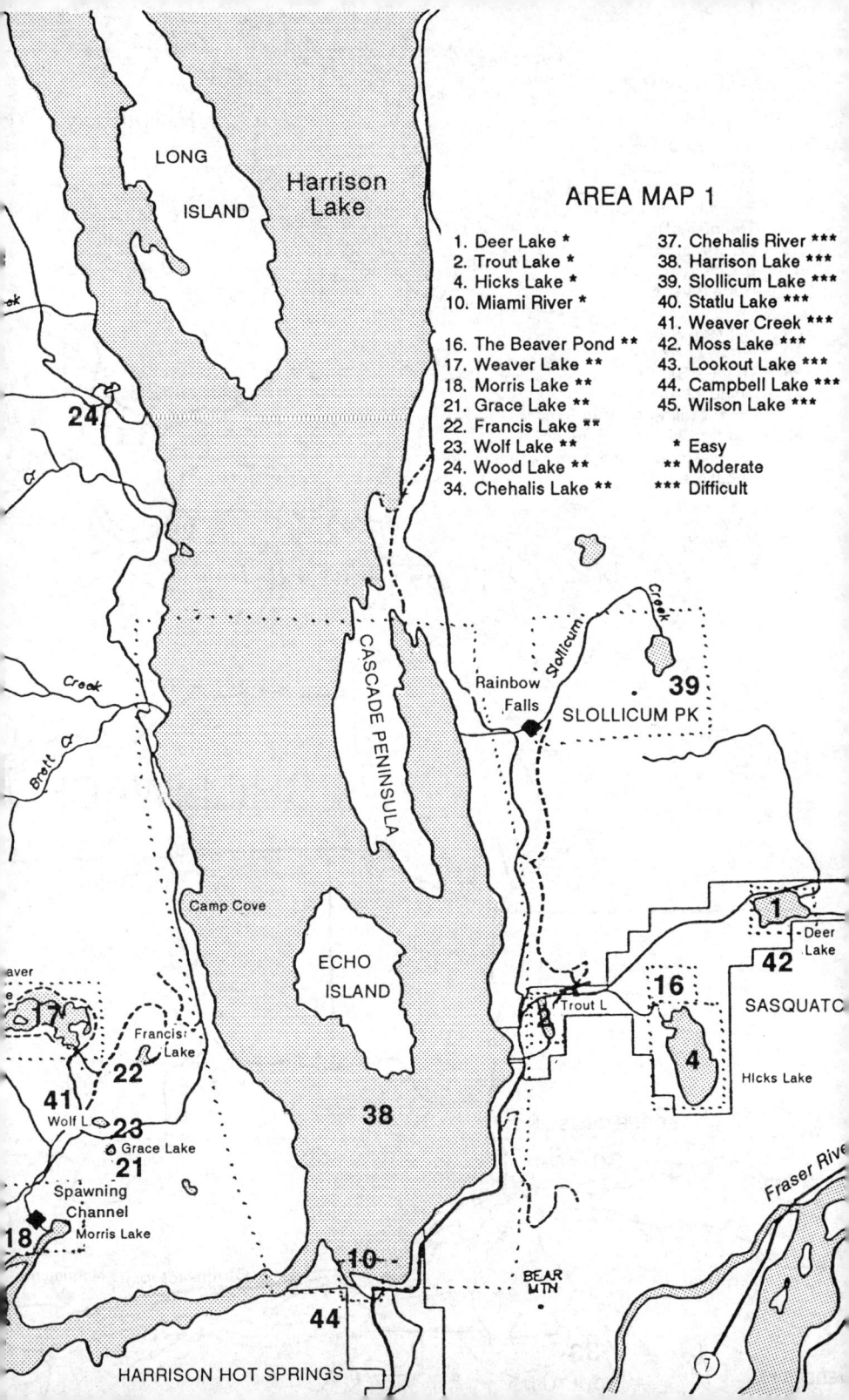

1. Deer Lake *
2. Trout Lake *
4. Hicks Lake *
10. Miami River *
16. The Beaver Pond **
17. Weaver Lake **
18. Morris Lake **
21. Grace Lake **
22. Francis Lake **
23. Wolf Lake **
24. Wood Lake **
34. Chehalis Lake **
37. Chehalis River ***
38. Harrison Lake ***
39. Slollicum Lake ***
40. Statlu Lake ***
41. Weaver Creek ***
42. Moss Lake ***
43. Lookout Lake ***
44. Campbell Lake ***
45. Wilson Lake ***

* Easy
** Moderate
*** Difficult

AREA MAP 2

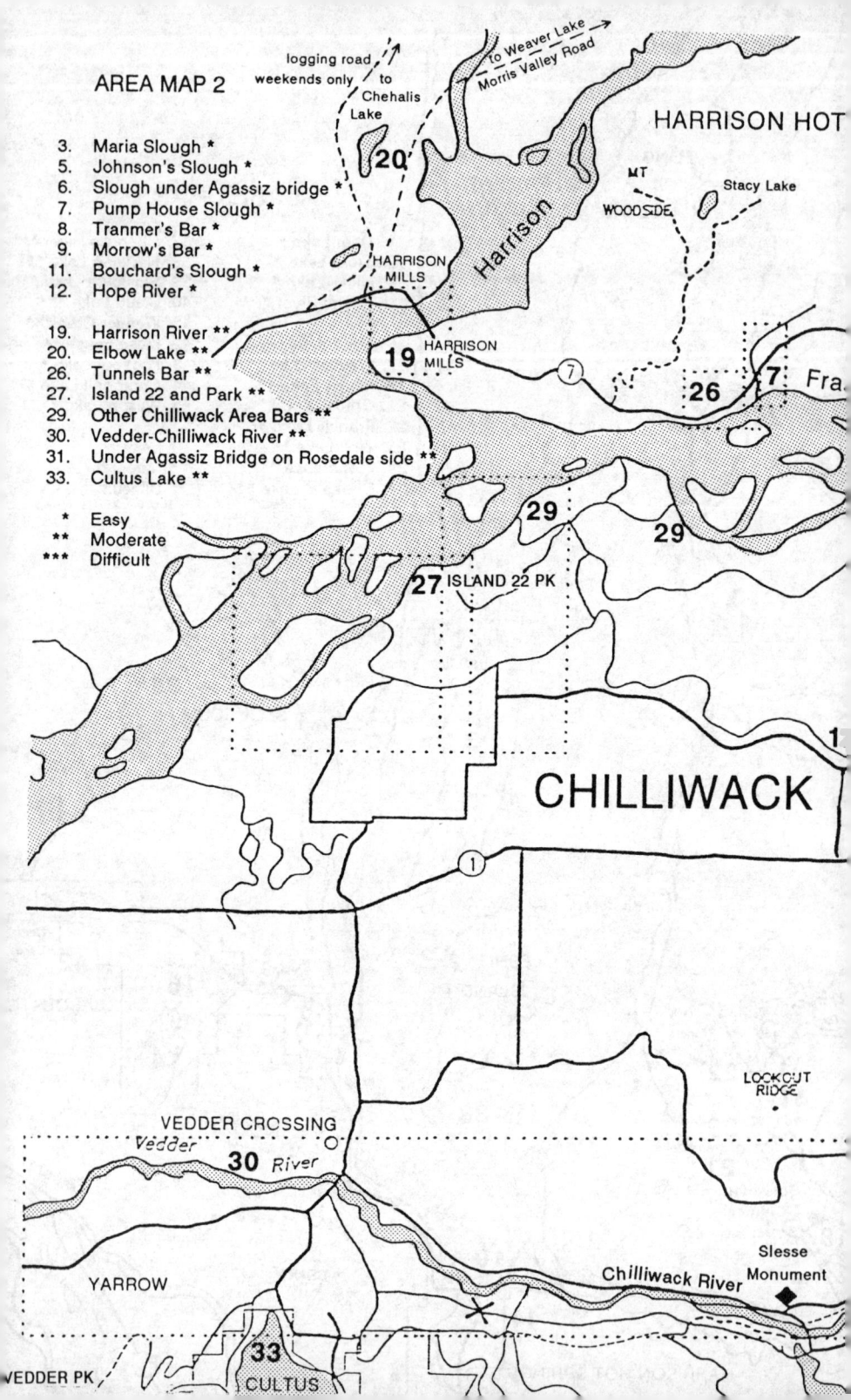

3. Maria Slough *
5. Johnson's Slough *
6. Slough under Agassiz bridge *
7. Pump House Slough *
8. Tranmer's Bar *
9. Morrow's Bar *
11. Bouchard's Slough *
12. Hope River *

19. Harrison River **
20. Elbow Lake **
26. Tunnels Bar **
27. Island 22 and Park **
29. Other Chilliwack Area Bars **
30. Vedder-Chilliwack River **
31. Under Agassiz Bridge on Rosedale side **
33. Cultus Lake **

* Easy
** Moderate
*** Difficult

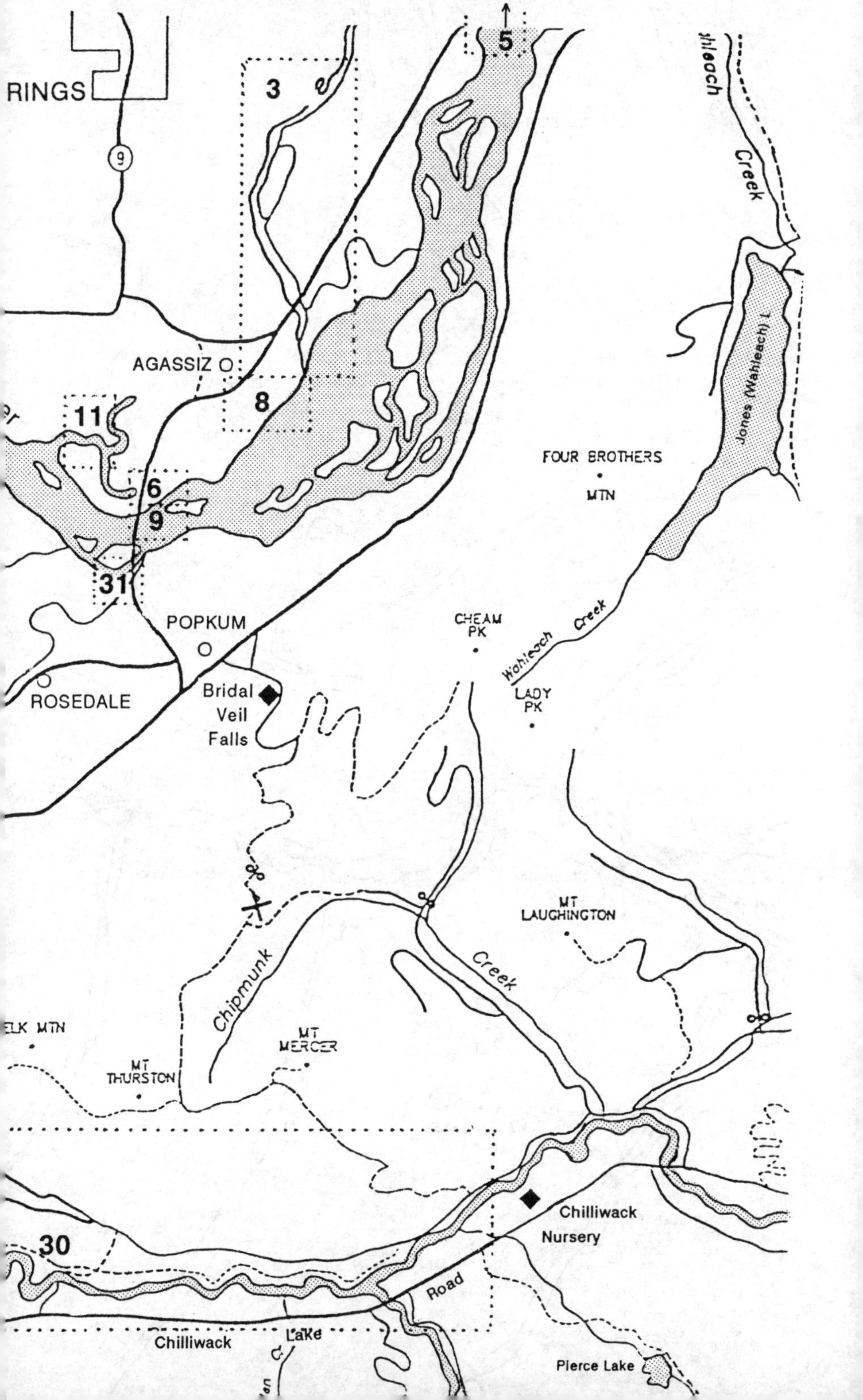
RINGS
9
3
5
AGASSIZ
8
11
6
9
31
POPKUM
ROSEDALE
Bridal
Veil
Falls
FOUR BROTHERS
MTN
CHEAM
PK
LADY
PK
Wahleach
Creek
Jones (Wahleach) L
Creek
MT
LAUGHINGTON
Chipmunk
Creek
ELK MTN
MT
THURSTON
MT
MERCER
Chilliwack
Nursery
30
Road
Chilliwack
Lake
Pierce Lake

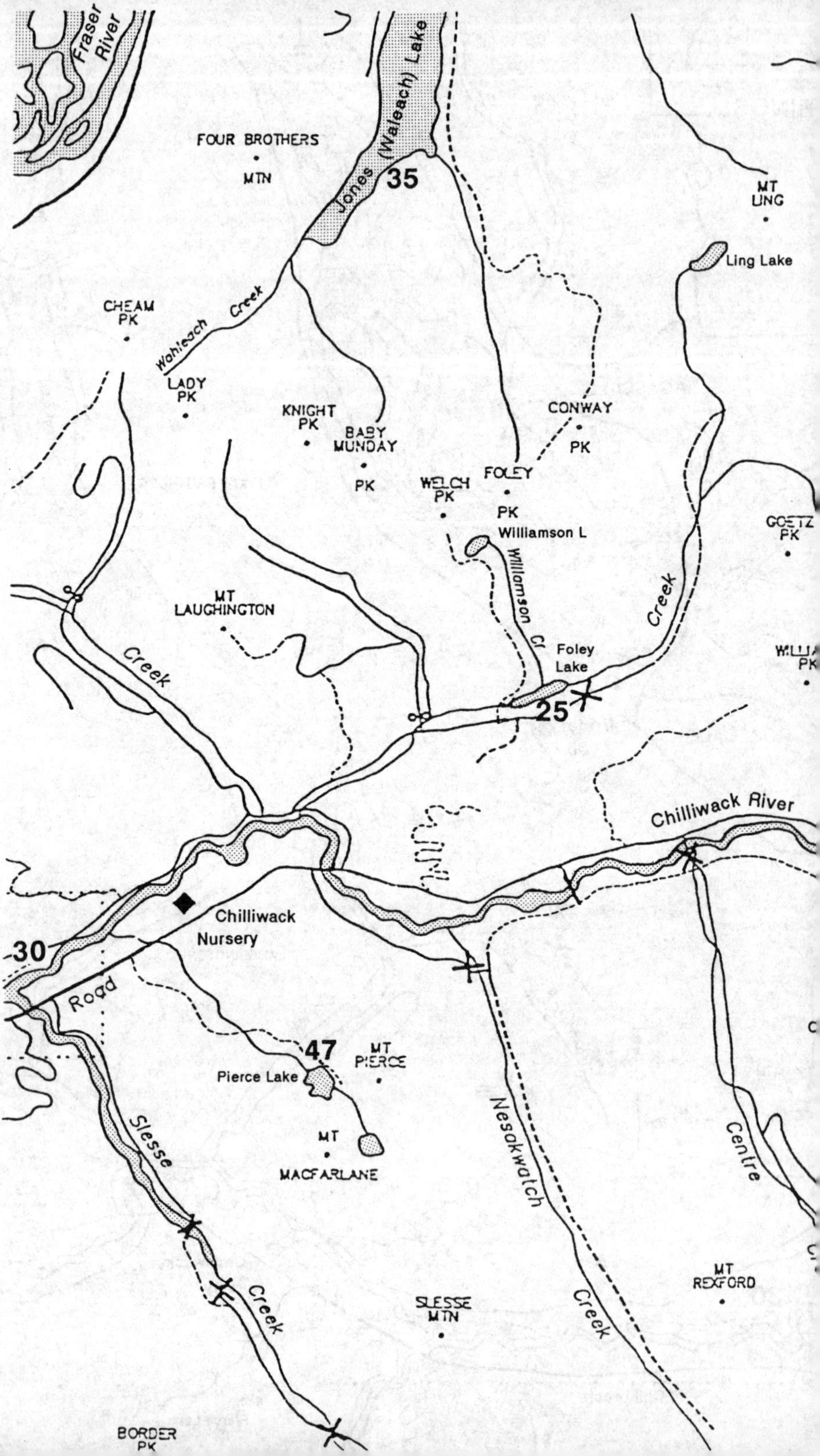

Fraser River
Jones (Waleach) Lake
FOUR BROTHERS MTN
35
MT LING
Ling Lake
CHEAM PK
Wahleach Creek
LADY PK
KNIGHT PK
BABY MUNDAY PK
CONWAY PK
WELCH PK
FOLEY PK
Williamson L
GOETZ PK
MT LAUGHINGTON
Williamson Cr
Creek
Creek
Foley Lake
25
Chilliwack River
Chilliwack Nursery
30
Road
47
MT PIERCE
Pierce Lake
MT MACFARLANE
Slesse
Nesakwatch
Centre
Creek
Creek
MT REXFORD
SLESSE MTN
BORDER PK

AREA MAP 3

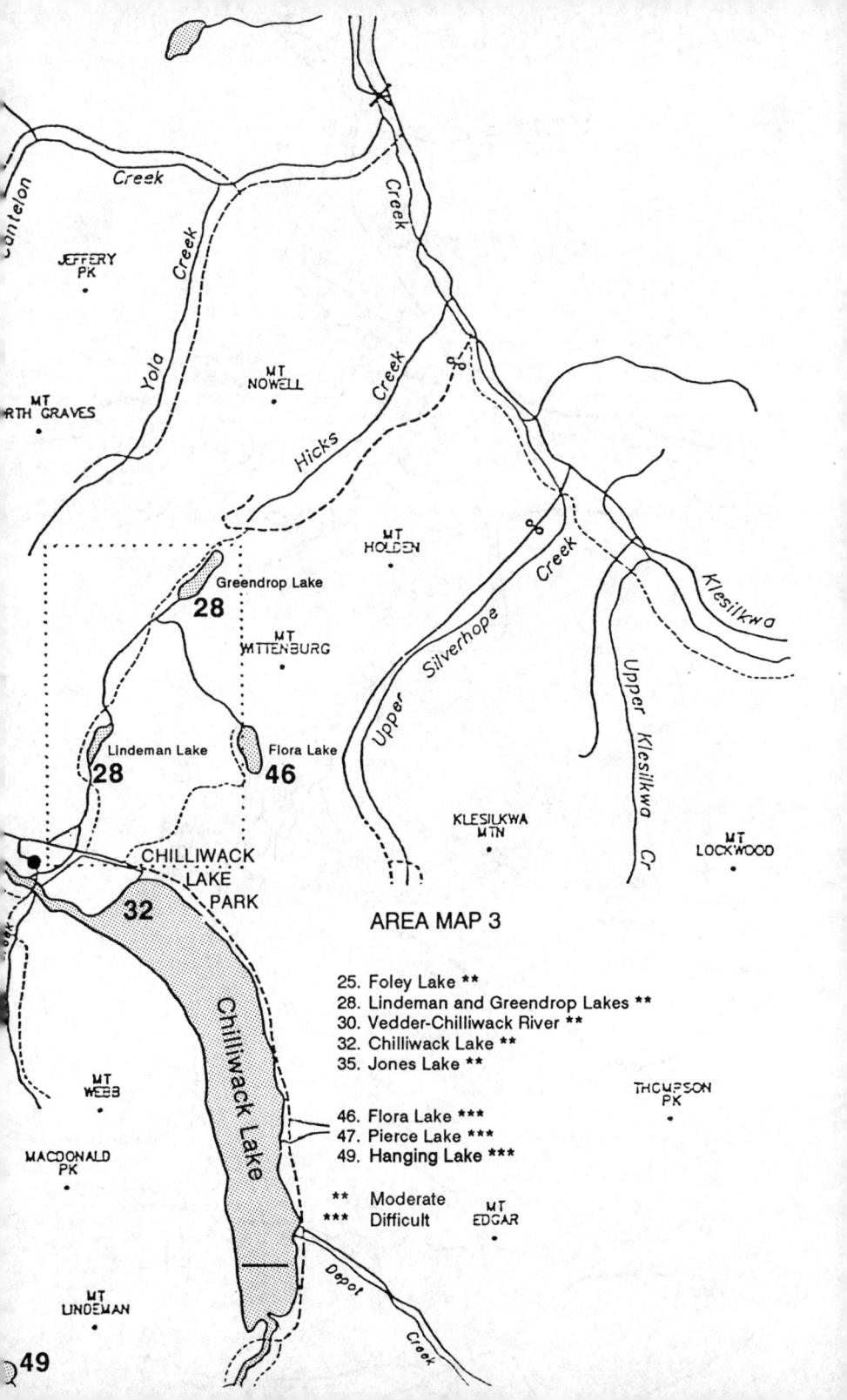

25. Foley Lake **
28. Lindeman and Greendrop Lakes **
30. Vedder-Chilliwack River **
32. Chilliwack Lake **
35. Jones Lake **

46. Flora Lake ***
47. Pierce Lake ***
49. Hanging Lake ***

　** Moderate
　*** Difficult

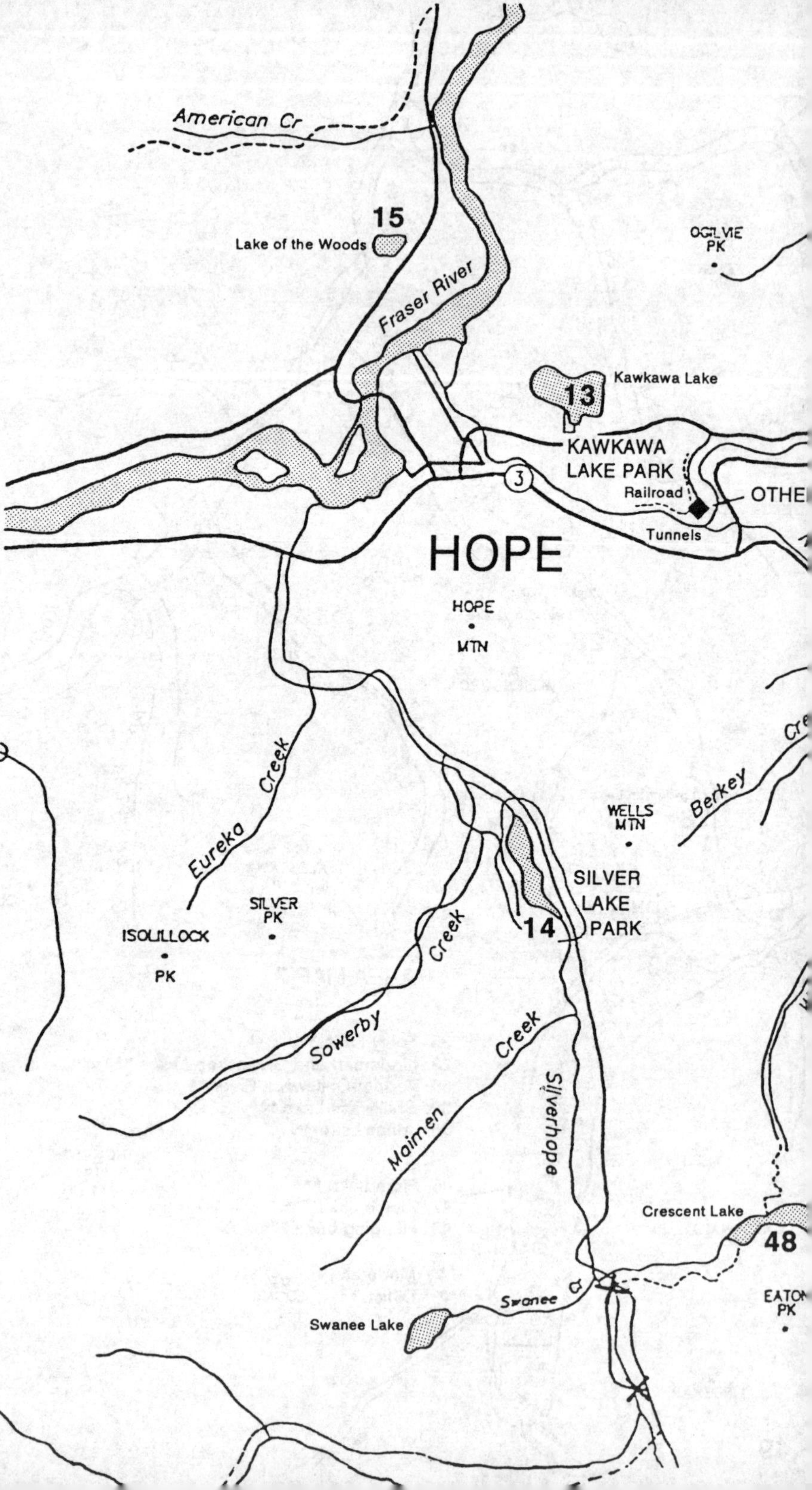
American Cr
15
Lake of the Woods
Fraser River
OGILVIE PK
Kawkawa Lake
13
KAWKAWA LAKE PARK
3
Railroad
OTHE
Tunnels
HOPE
HOPE MTN
Eureka Creek
Cre
Berkey
WELLS MTN
SILVER LAKE PARK
14
SILVER PK
ISOLILLOCK PK
Sowerby Creek
Maimen Creek
Silverhope
Crescent Lake
48
EATON PK
Swanee Lake
Swanee Cr

AREA MAP 4

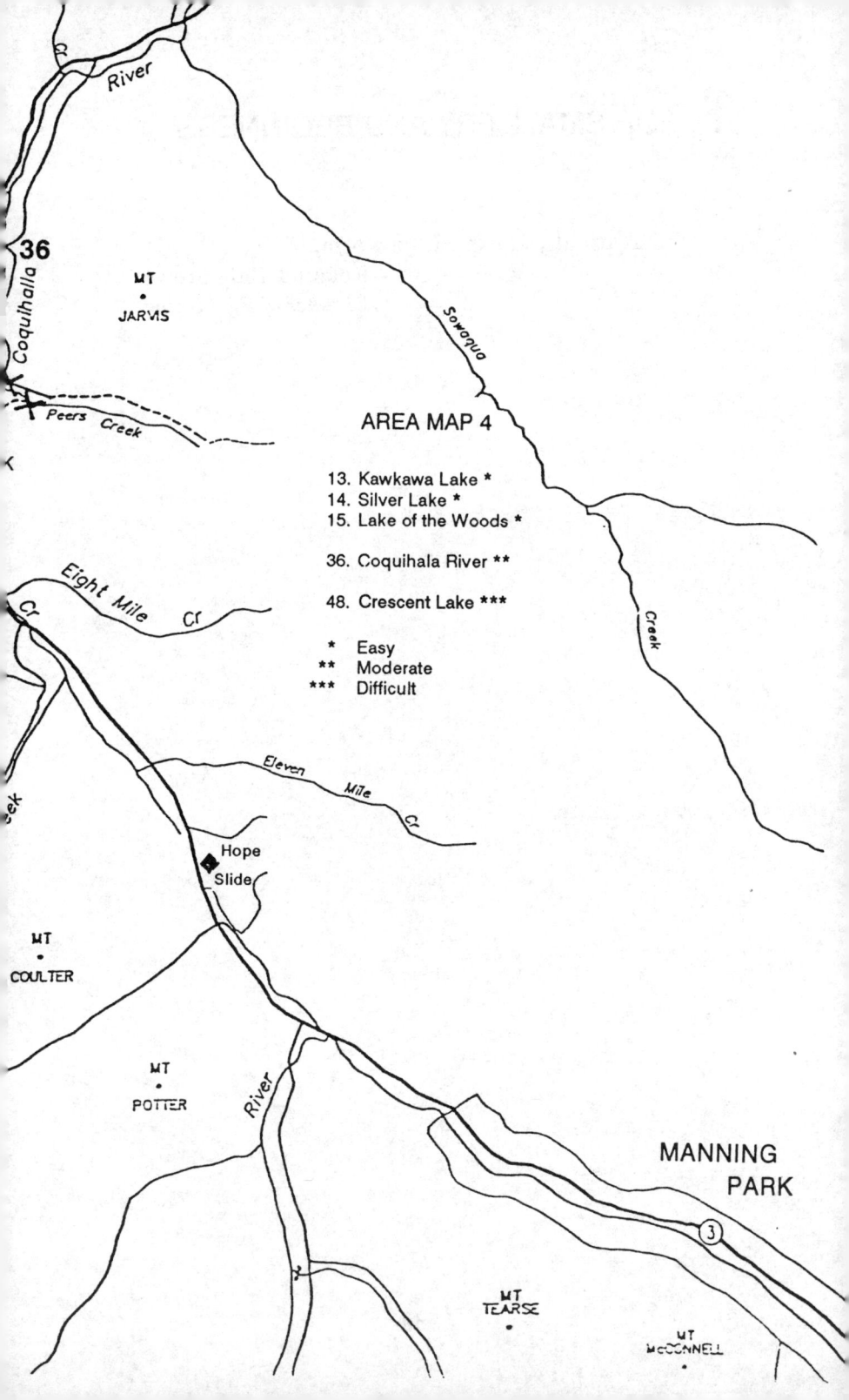

13. Kawkawa Lake *
14. Silver Lake *
15. Lake of the Woods *

36. Coquihala River **

48. Crescent Lake ***

*   Easy
** Moderate
*** Difficult

1 FOR SMALL FRY AND BEGINNERS

"It usually starts with a worm..."
—Roderick Haig Brown
A Primer of Fly Fishing

INTRODUCTION

Fishing is one of our oldest and most popular activities. This is especially true in British Columbia, a land blessed with numerous lakes and streams. Some of these fishing spots are within a 1 or 2 hour drive of Vancouver, in the Upper Fraser Valley.

For many years I have fished the lakes, streams, rivers and sloughs of the Upper Fraser Valley with considerable success. This little book details the best of these fishing spots.

Some of these areas are better known to me than others. Those that are well-known have detailed sketches showing where to fish. With the exception of the Vedder-Chilliwack River, the Agassiz and Harrison areas have the best fishing possibilities in the upper valley, thus my emphasis on the north shore.

This book is divided into four parts. Part I is for small fry and beginners—children and adults learning the art of fishing. These are the areas that consistently produce fish, are easy to get to and are easily fished from shore or with a small boat. I have emphasized this section, since many people will be content to limit their fishing to these spots.

Some fishermen, however, might want a greater challenge. Thus, Part II is for the knowledgeable and experienced. These are the areas that require greater ability, knowledge and experience to catch fish.

Part III is for the highly skilled and dedicated. These are the most difficult spots to fish, requiring the greatest ability combined with stamina and endurance. Most people will not want to fish these areas but the adventuresome, dedicated and skilled may give them a try.

Part IV describes the game fish found in the Upper Fraser Valley along with some of their habits. This is especially relevant for beginners or visitors from other provinces or other countries.

There are general maps of the Agassiz, Harrison, Chilliwack and Hope areas. On these maps the fishing spots are marked by number. These numbers refer to the sequential numbering of the lakes and streams found in the outline. The numerous maps are drawn so that north is at the top of the page. This is standard practice in maps and should help orient the reader.

In sharing my best fishing spots, I urge anglers to adhere to ethical standards. Please take your litter with you since no one wants to fish near garbage. Treat private property, as well as your fellow anglers, with respect. Obey the regulations and check them closely for closures and special rules.

Above all, fishing should be fun. I hope my little guide opens a window of fishing opportunities for many people from three to ninety-nine. After all, one is never too young or too old to go fishing. Tight lines and good luck!

Richard Probert,
Agassiz, B.C.

LEGEND FOR MAPS

PAVED ROAD ═══════
GRAVEL ROAD ═══════
TRAIL — — — — — —
BCFS CAMPSITE ▲
ROCKS   XXX
BIG TREES   🌲 🌲
BRIDGE ⊐──⊏
STREAM ────→
HOUSE OR BARN ▨
RAILWAY ┼┼┼┼┼┼┼┼┼┼┼
GAS PIPELINE   -G-G-G-G-G-
BEAVER LODGE   ✳
LOGS ≡

1 DEER LAKE

Deer Lake is in Sasquatch Park, 12 kilometers or 7.5 miles northeast of Harrison Hot Springs. The lake is 54 hectares or 133 acres in area and is stocked with rainbow and cutthroat trout to 3 pounds, though smaller fish are the norm.

This lake is ideal for children and beginners, since the fish are plentiful and easy to catch. The fish in Deer Lake are nearly always obliging if you know when and where to fish and what to use.

I first fished Deer Lake as a fifteen year old boy in September, 1961. At that time, there was still logging in the area and a gate near the Deer Lake turnoff blocked cars. My companions and I hiked in from Wahleach over the power line road into Hicks Lake, then into Deer Lake via a logging road. We camped at the east end of the lake on a sandbar. Exploring the area, we found a battered old wooden boat, which we promptly loaded with gear and paddled to a point of land near the west end. This is the area marked "the point" on my first map.

Along the way I caught a 3 pound cutthroat trout trolling a willow leaf and worm. The big trout bent my little rod until I thought it would snap. Somehow, I managed to land the giant cutthroat while both my companions bailed water with pots! We spent the rest of the weekend camped on the point, catching numerous 12- to 14-inch trout. These trout seemed small compared with the giant 3 pounder caught earlier. This gives you some idea of the fishing thirty years ago. We were just boys—imagine the catch of a seasoned angler!

I fished Deer Lake sporadically during the early 1970s. When I started fishing again, in 1984, Deer Lake was a favorite choice. By then the logging was finished and a provincial park had been created around Hicks, Deer and Trout lakes.

My notes for 1984 indicate that I caught numerous trout over 12 inches, the biggest being 16 inches, with quite a few 13, 14, and 15 inchers. Since then fishing pressure has reduced the average fish size to under 12 inches or 30 centimeters. However, there are still many 16- to 18-inch trout waiting to be caught. There are just enough big trout in Deer Lake to entice the angler year after year.

My notes also indicate that the best months to fish Deer Lake are April, May and June, then September, October and November. The summer months still produce fish but they are occasionally soft. However, many people fish the lake during July and August. Just remember to fish early and late in the day.

As for tackle, a small trout rod and reel will be sufficient. Indeed, a small trout rod will be sufficient for nearly all areas mentioned in this book. The exceptions to this are for fishing

MAP 1   DEER LAKE WEST END AND POINT

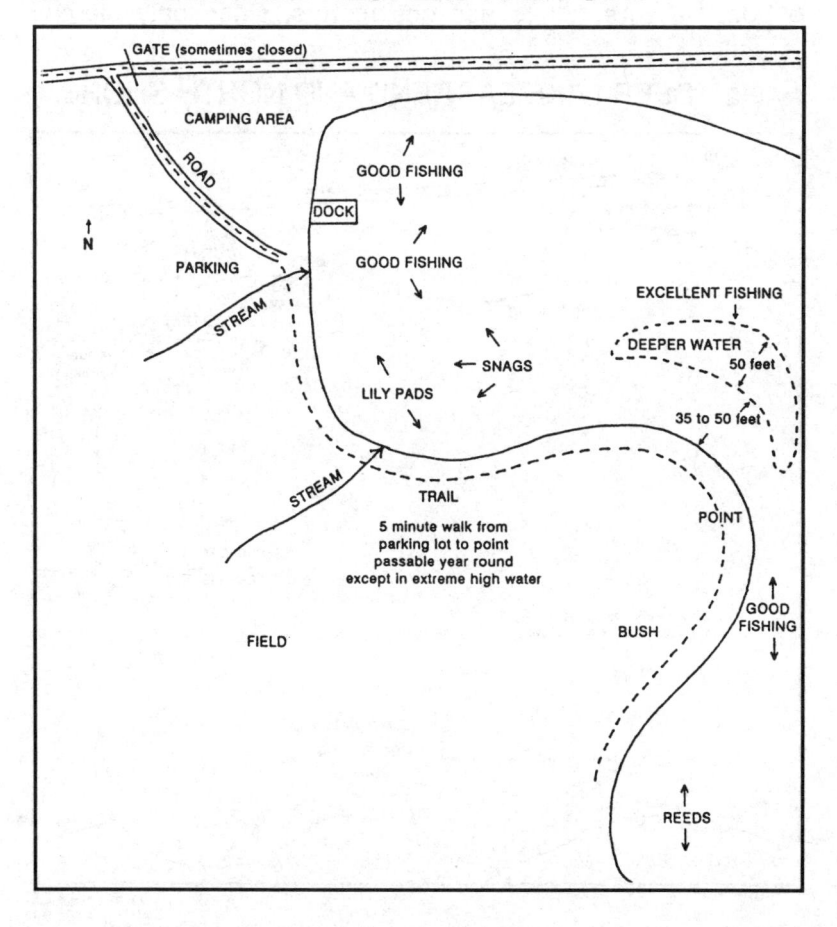

steelhead and coho, in which case a larger rod and reel and heavier line are needed. Personally, I prefer graphite rods, since each strike or hit is easily seen and felt with this kind of flexible rod. Six or eight test line is appropriate for most lakes and streams in the Upper Fraser Valley. The exception is for salmon and steelhead, when heavier line, perhaps 12 pound test, is needed.

I generally use worms when fishing from the shore of Deer Lake. This just seems like a worm lake. Salmon eggs can also be effective. Trolling a Doc Spratly, royal coachman or black gnat fly also catches fish. And, if flies fail, try a wedding band lure and worm. This will almost certainly produce results.

Deer Lake has full camping facilities nearby. If you bring a boat be sure not to use gas motors, since only electric

MAP 2 DEER LAKE EAST END AND NORTH SHORE

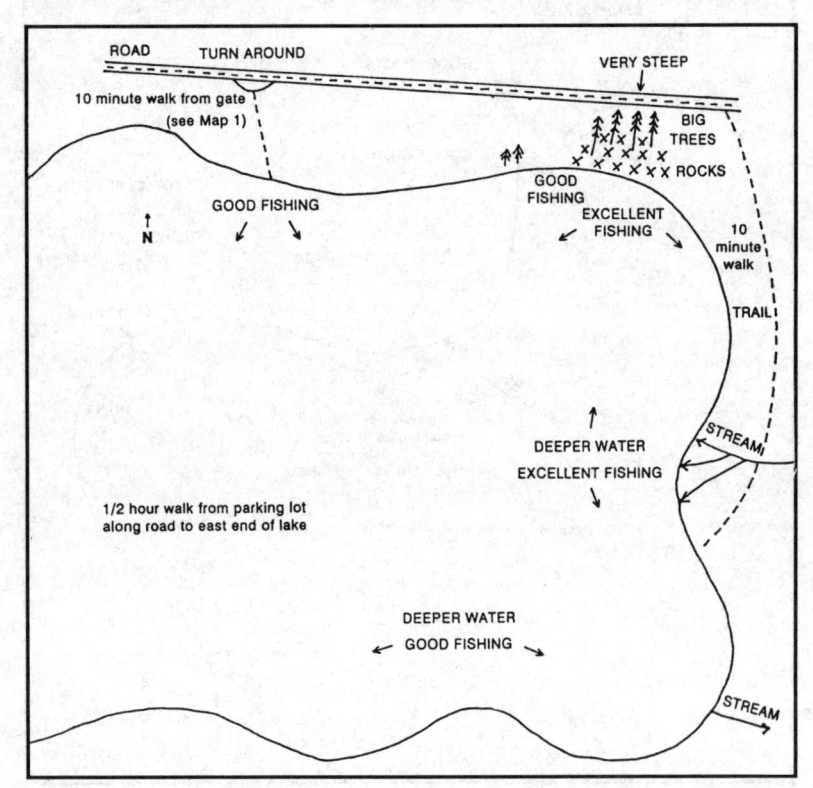

motors are allowed. The trail to the point is passable year round, except in extremely high water in the spring. As for worms or salmon eggs, they can be purchased in Agassiz and Harrison Hot Springs at various locations.

If you are looking for a good spot to introduce children to fishing, I heartily recommend Deer Lake. With yearly stockings, there will always be fish to catch. Children and beginners don't usually care about the size of the fish as long as there is plenty of action which Deer Lake provides.

NOTES: _____

2 TROUT LAKE

This little lake is 12 hectares or 30 acres in area and is in Sasquatch Park 7 kilometers or 4.4 miles northeast of Harrison Hot Springs. Trout Lake is best in February, just after the ice melts, March, April, May and September, October and November. A word of advice: if you plan to walk through the marsh to fish near the stream on the east side be sure to wear waterproof boots. This is a very wet area.

Trout Lake has mainly small fish. Indeed, my largest fish was a 14-inch cutthroat trout caught 25 years ago. There are still a few bigger fish in Trout Lake, enough to entice the angler. Note: no power boats are allowed.

NOTES: _____
_____
_____

MAP 3   TROUT LAKE

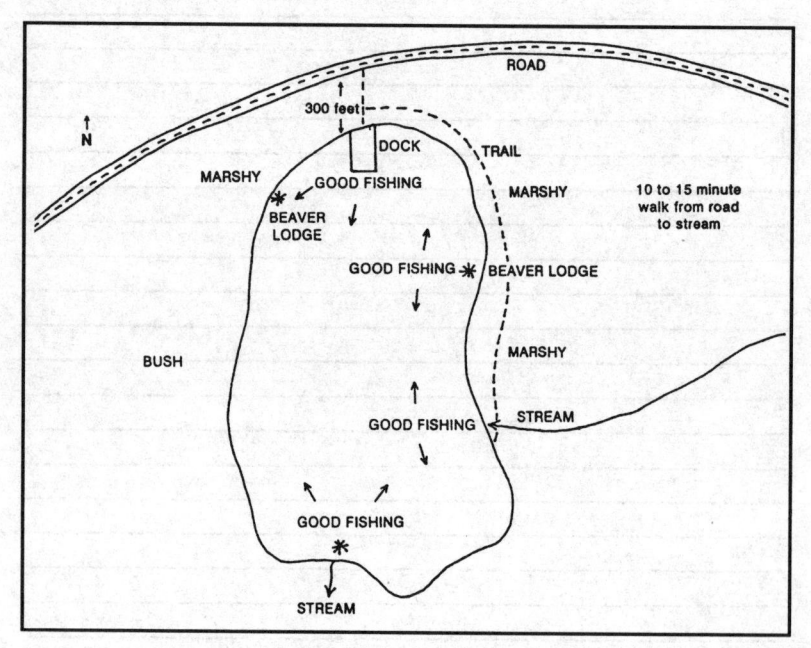

MAP 3a MARIA SLOUGH OVERVIEW

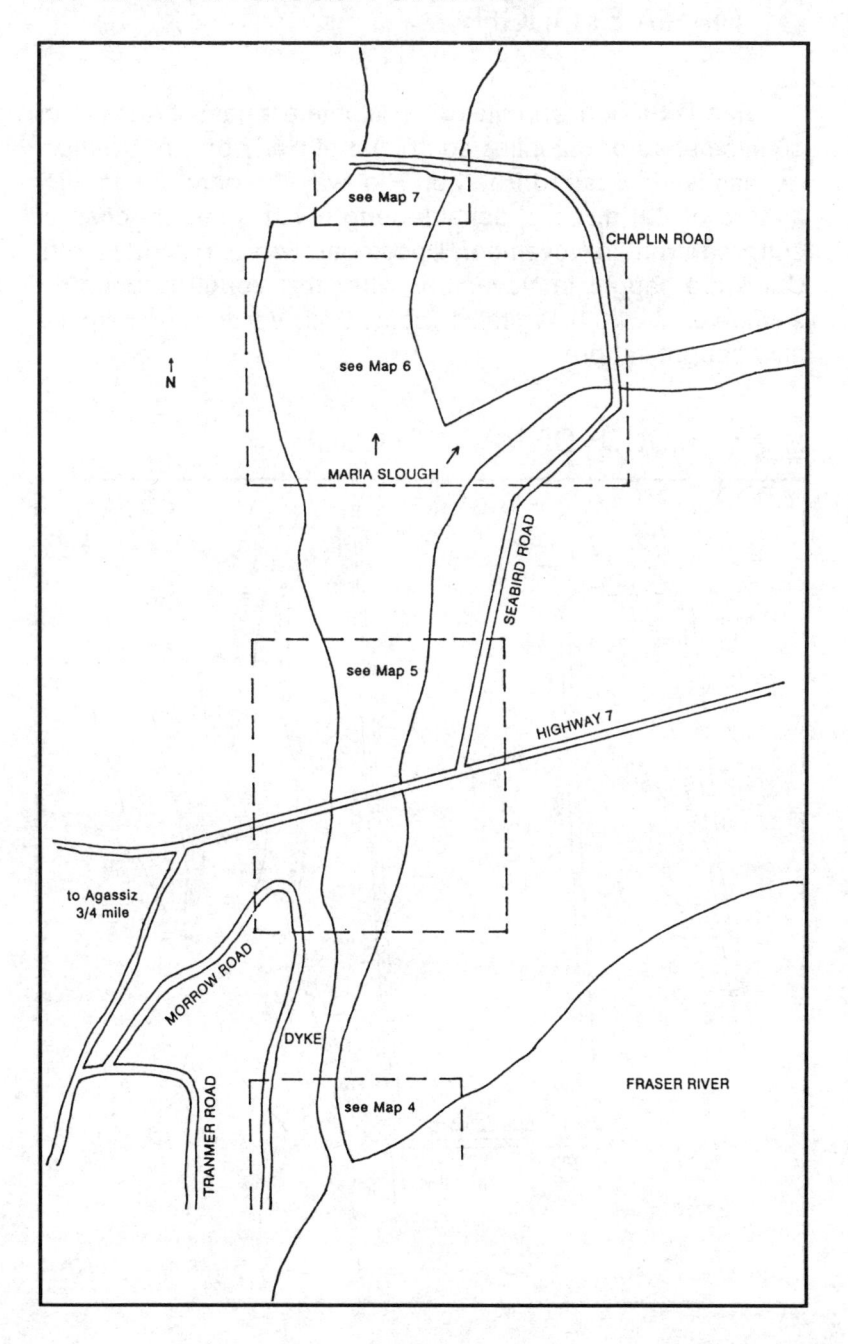

3 MARIA SLOUGH

Maria Slough is 1 mile or 1.6 kilometers east of Agassiz or 10 kilometers or 6.2 miles southeast of Harrison Hot Springs. Access is via Seabird Road off Highway 7. There are 11 kilometers or 6.8 miles of fishable length with good catches of cutthroat trout in November, December, February, and March. Coho are caught in November, after the slough is open for salmon on the 16th. Whitefish, some Dolly Varden and carp are also caught in here.

MAP 4   MOUTH OF MARIA SLOUGH

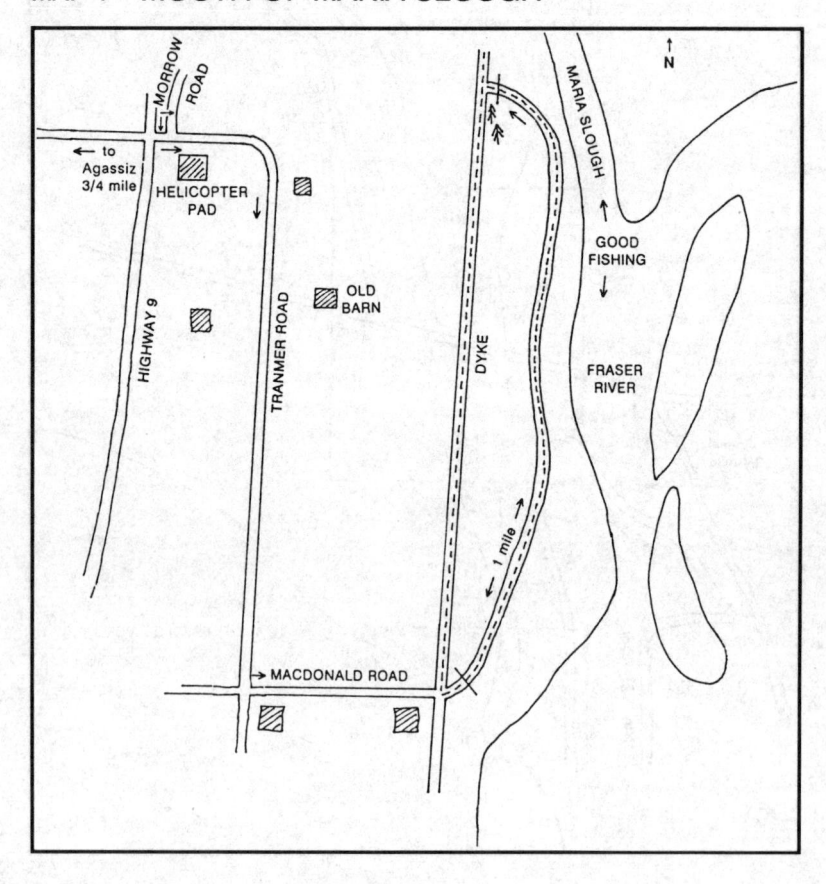

My first fish was caught in Maria Slough. It was a small bullhead and I proudly carried it home for my mother, aunt and grandmother to see.

Now, there are cutthroat trout in Maria Slough year round. The sea-run cutthroat go to the Fraser estuary in the spring, returning to their birthplace with the salmon in the fall. It is the sea-run cutthroat that fishermen prize, since they can reach 5 pounds or more.

Fishermen also prize coho salmon. The Maria Slough run for coho usually starts in the second week of October and goes

MAP 5   MARIA SLOUGH NEAR HIGHWAY 7

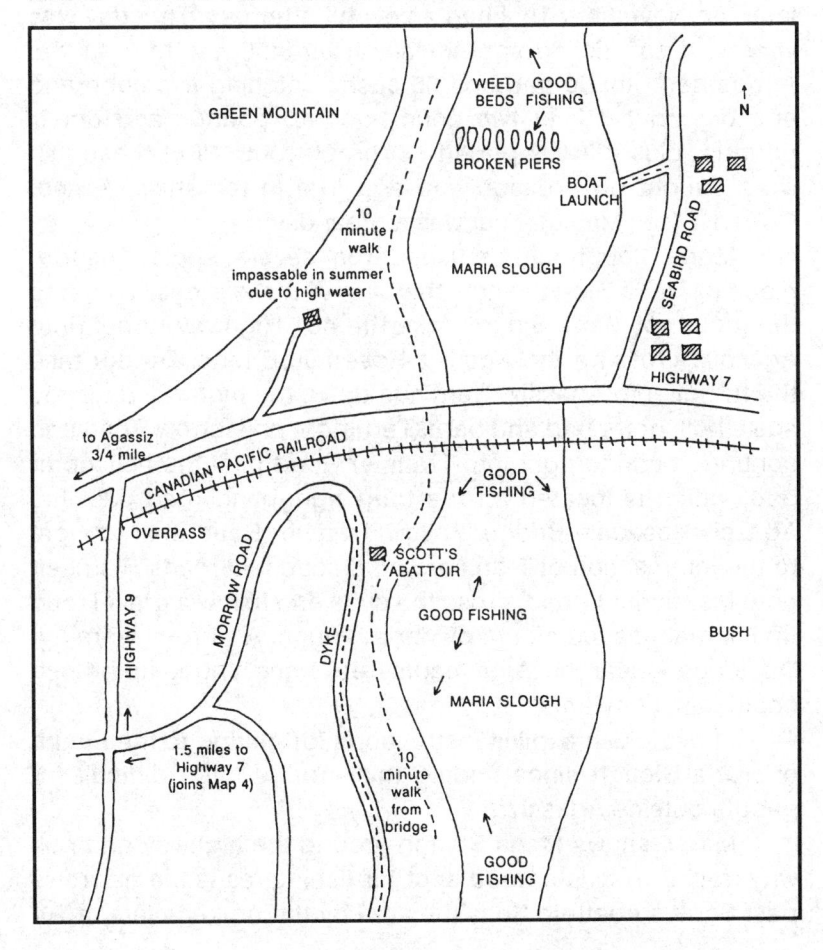

right into the middle of December. I have heard of fishermen taking silver coho in late December, but these are exceptions.

For best results, try worms, roe, flies or lures for cutthroat trout, Dolly Varden and whitefish and lures or salmon roe for coho. The best lures are: bacon and egg, crocodile and coho lures. These can be purchased in Agassiz.

My notes reveal that 1985 was a good year for fishing Maria Slough. One memorable day in November, the 5th to be exact, I fished at Culvert Number 2 (see Map 7) and caught two beautiful sea-run cutthroat trout—one 2 1/2 pounds, the other 1 1/2 pounds. I caught them on roe between 11:30 and 12:30 during a minor solunar period, just before a storm. A few days later, on November 19, I had an even better day. That day was very cold so I fished sporadically from 8:30 A.M. to 3:30 P.M. Altogether, I made perhaps 35 casts, catching five coho and one big trout. I kept two coho—one 10 pounds and one 7 pounds, plus a 1 1/2 pound cutthroat trout. All of these fish were caught on a bacon and egg lure in the shallows near Culvert 1 (see Map 6). That was a great day!

Maria Slough can be fished from several spots. The four maps of Maria Slough show the best of these areas. To get to the mouth of Maria Slough take the 401 Highway turnoff into Agassiz, crossing the Agassiz-Rosedale Bridge. Do not take the turnoff into Agassiz. Continue down the highway until you see a helicopter pad and barn. Turn right on Morrow Road and continue bearing right into Tranmer Road past the helicopter pad, which is located on the third right-hand road past the Agassiz-Rosedale Bridge. Follow Tranmer Road until you get to the intersection of Tranmer and Macdonald roads. Turn left onto Macdonald Road, cross the dyke and follow a gravel road until it reaches the mouth of Maria Slough. A word of warning. Do not park near the large maple tree, since a hung up branch could fall at any time.

I have given explicit instructions for getting to the mouth of Maria Slough since finding this area is often difficult for people outside Agassiz.

Map 5 shows Maria Slough around the highway and railway tracks. This is a good spot for fishing, as is the narrrows past Scott's Abattoir. So is the area by the broken piers, a 10-

minute walk from the road. Park your car by the side of the road but be sure to lock it and keep your valuables out of sight.

A humorous incident occurred at the railway bridge. A friend of mine caught a fat 14-inch cutthroat trout and left it on the bank. He was busy casting, hoping for a coho and suddenly realized that he was quite a distance from his fish. He looked back in time to see a large sea gull swimming away with his fish!

Map 6 shows Maria Slough past Culvert Number 1. Parking is a problem since you must park by the side of the road. However, this is a good spot to fish, with numerous places along the bank.

MAP 6   MARIA SLOUGH NEAR CULVERT NUMBER 1

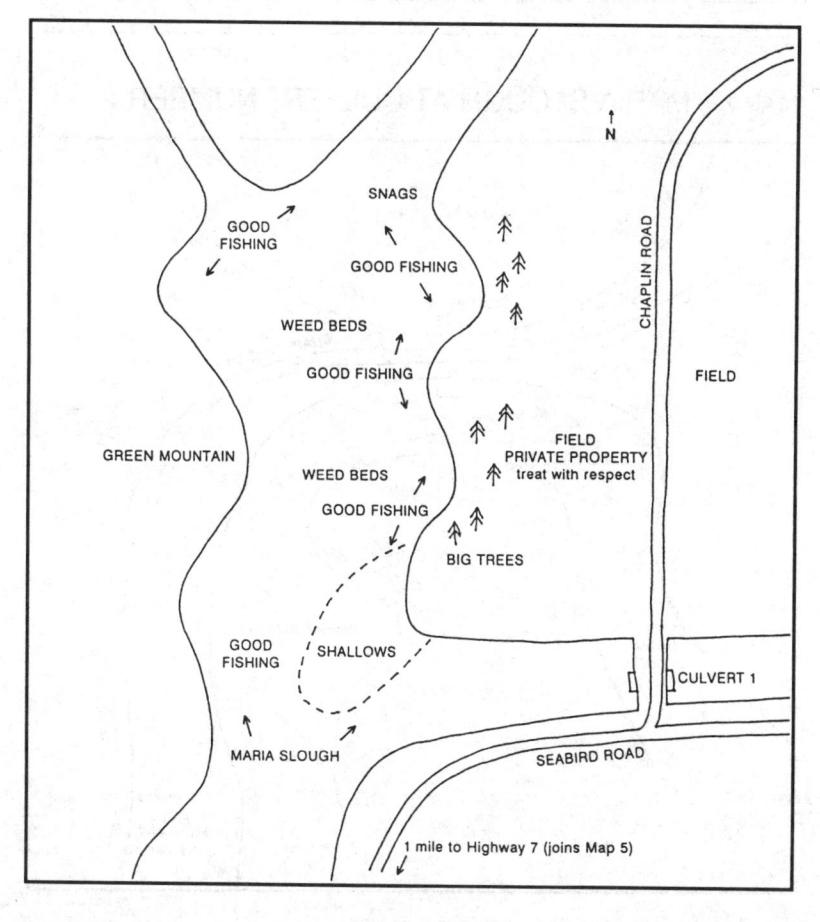

For good fishing in low water, walk onto the bar marked the shallows.

Finally, Map 7 shows the Culvert Number 2. This is a favorite haunt of youngsters and seasoned pros alike. Watch for the snags. Maria Slough can provide many memorable angling experiences.

NOTES: _____
_____
_____
_____
_____
_____
_____

MAP 7   MARIA SLOUGH AT CULVERT NUMBER 2

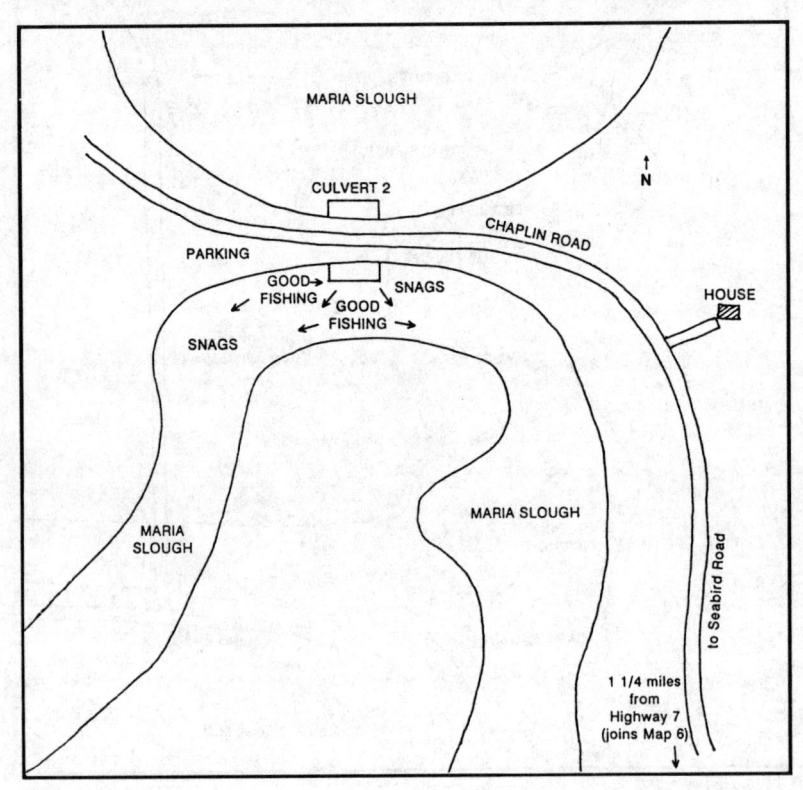

4 HICKS LAKE

Hicks Lake is in Sasquatch Park 11 kilometers or 6.8 miles northeast of Harrison Hot Springs. The lake is 104 hectares or 257 acres in area with full camping facilities nearby. The lake is stocked with rainbow and cutthroat trout and kokanee.

At one time, in the 1930s, Hicks Lake was perhaps the best trout lake in the Fraser Valley. That was before logging and before the water level was raised by a dam.

My father fished Hicks Lake sixty years ago. He walked in from Wahleach on a trail through tall timbers. With local help

MAP 8   HICKS LAKE

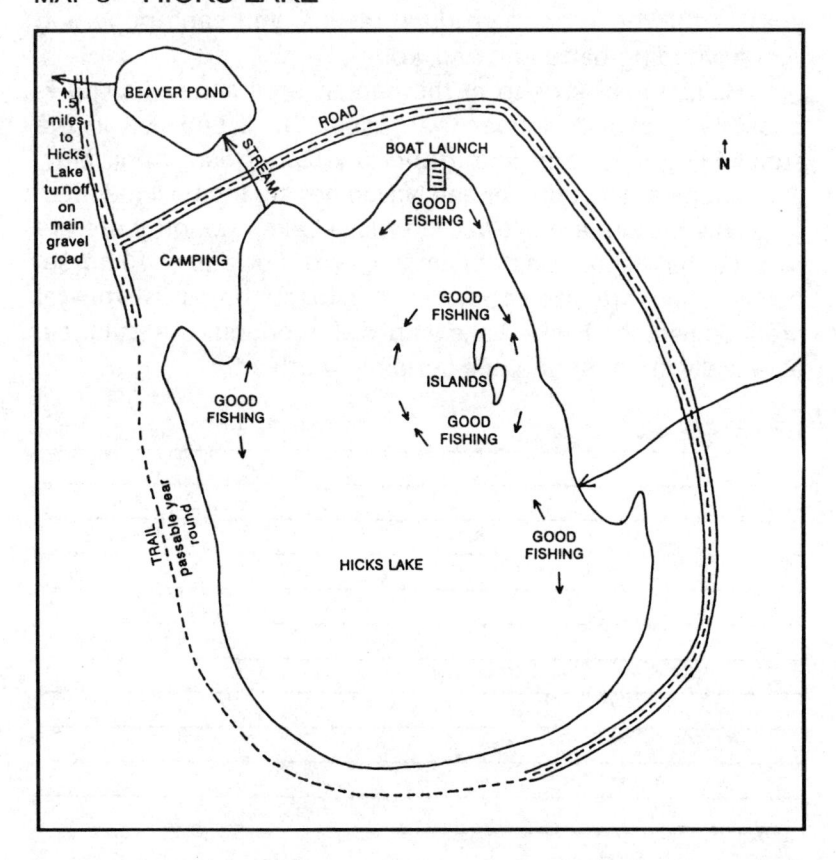

he packed in two wooden boats, which he then used for a guiding business on the lake. I have pictures from that era showing large rainbows in the 2 to 5 pound range. These fish were caught by fly fishing.

My mother remembers one fish in particular. It was a large rainbow that followed the boat but would never strike a fly. This fish regularly followed the boat, testing my father's patience. Could this be the same fish as the 17 pounder caught in the spring of 1956?

Hicks Lake is more difficult to fish from the shore than Deer Lake. The best spots for shore fishing are along the northeast shore in the bays and opposite the islands. Near the outlet of the stream flowing into the Beaver Pond is also a good spot.

Most people fish Hicks Lake with a boat, trolling flies, lures or a willow leaf and worm. A wide variety of flies and lures are used. If these don't produce results, you can't go wrong with a wedding band lure and worm.

Hicks Lake is deep at the center, so summer fishing is possible—just fish deeper than usual. Or, if you fish in the summer try early and late in the day. Otherwise, April, May, June, September, October and November are the best months.

Gas motors are allowed on Hicks Lake, though there are restrictions on the size of the motor—7.5 kilowatts or 10 horsepower. There are also sandy beaches for sunbathing if you get tired of fishing. Hicks Lake can still produce fine catches, especially in the spring. It's certainly worth a try.

NOTES: _____
_____
_____
_____
_____
_____
_____
_____
_____
_____
_____
_____

5 JOHNSON'S SLOUGH

Johnson's Slough is 14.4 kilometers or 9 miles east of Agassiz, beside Highway 7. It has runs of cutthroat trout, coho and spring jacks. My notes reveal that August is a good month to fish for jacks. Indeed, last August, I caught a 17-inch spring jack. Aside from this, September and October are good months for cutthroat trout and coho, while April, May and June are good months for cutthroat trout. For best results, try worms, salmon eggs, lures or flies.

NOTES: _____

MAP 9   JOHNSON'S SLOUGH

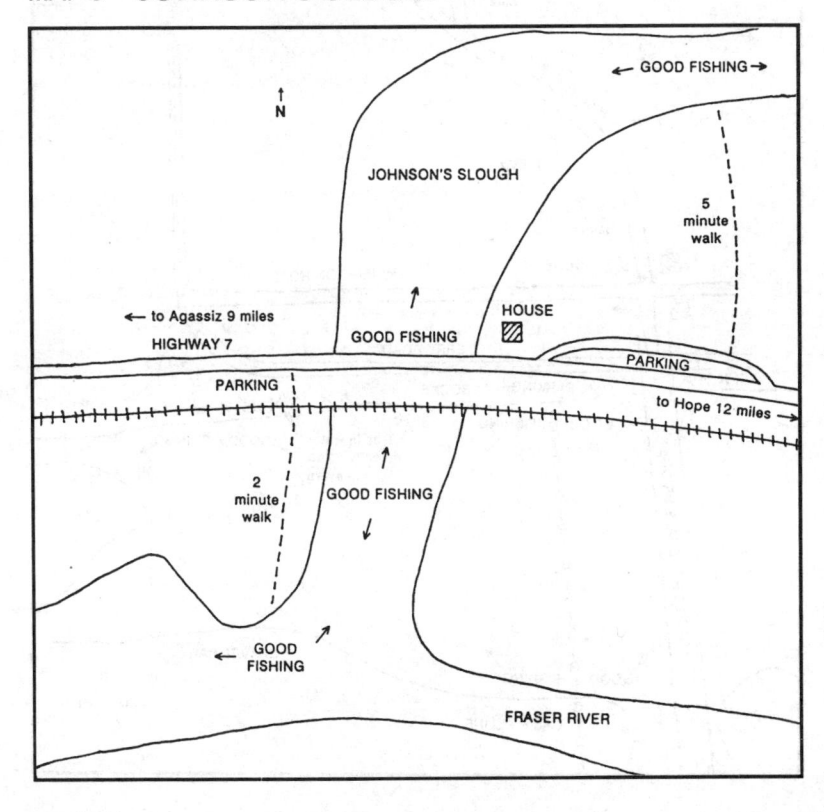

6 SLOUGH UNDER AGASSIZ BRIDGE

This slough used to be a real hot spot thirty years ago, with excellent catches of cutthroat trout, coho and even a few steelhead. It can still produce fair catches of cutthroat trout in September, October, November, December, February, March and April. Occasionally sturgeon are also caught in August.

To get to this spot, take the Highway 401 turnoff into Agassiz and cross the Agassiz-Rosedale Bridge. Turn right on

MAP 10 SLOUGH UNDER AGASSIZ BRIDGE

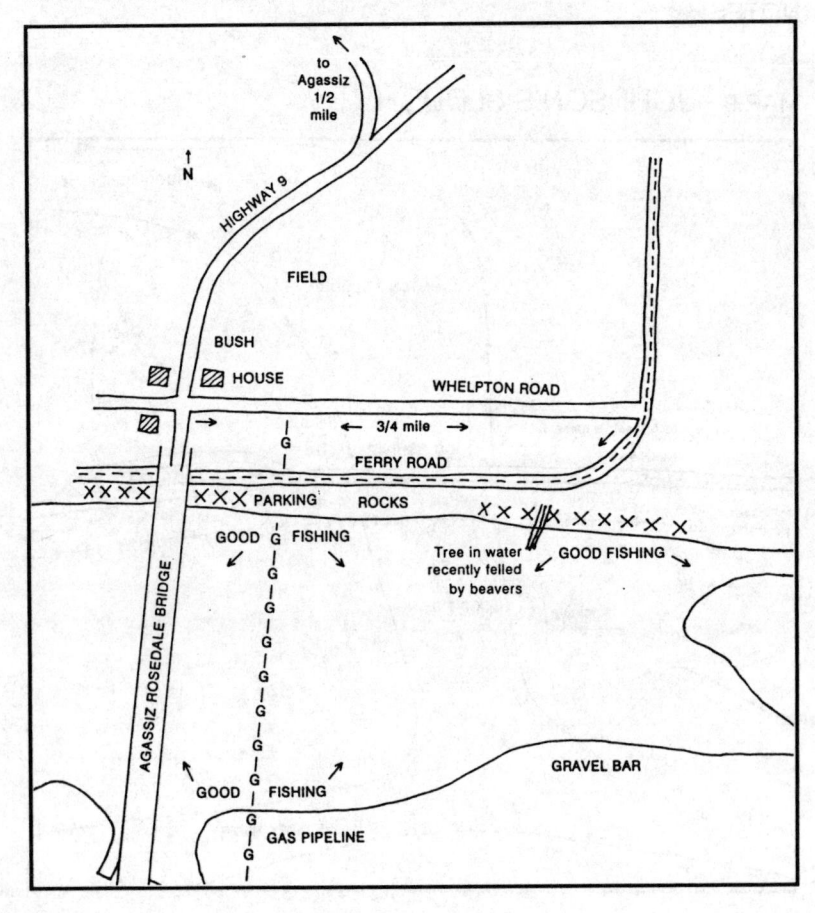

34

Whelpton Road the first road past the bridge. This is not very far from the end of the bridge so be alert. A house near some woods on the right-hand side is a good landmark. Cross the dyke, then proceed straight down until reaching the end of the road. Turn right onto Ferry Road which is a gravel road and proceed until you are near the bridge. Park here.

Most people fish near their parked cars. However, if you walk east for ten or fifteen minutes a good spot can be reached. You must climb over rocks part of the way but the effort is worthwhile. Look for a flat rock halfway down the shore along the rocks. Fish here for good catches of cutthroat trout. December, January and February are the best months for this spot.

My notes indicate that cutthroat trout to 2 pounds or more can be caught in these waters. I have caught a few 2 pounders with numerous 13 to 16 inchers. Sometimes the fishing is slow but patience usually rewards the angler with a fish or two.

This slough is ideal for fly fishing with lots of room for casting. I have seen fishermen with belly boats catching quite a few fish. For those who don't know, a belly boat is an inflatable seat, which enables the angler who is well insulated to fish the more inaccessible areas in small lakes or sloughs. This is an ideal way to fish since it provides the convenience of a boat with the mobility of someone fishing from shore.

NOTES: _____
_____
_____
_____
_____
_____
_____
_____
_____
_____
_____
_____
_____

7 PUMP HOUSE SLOUGH

This little slough is 8 kilometers or 5 miles west of Agassiz near Highway 7 at the base of Mount Woodside. The Pump House Slough has been a continuous producer year after year with fair numbers of cutthroat trout and a few coho in the fall. My notes indicate that November, December, February and March are the best months for this slough. I have caught quite a few coho jacks in November and numerous trout in December and February.

MAP 11 PUMP HOUSE SLOUGH

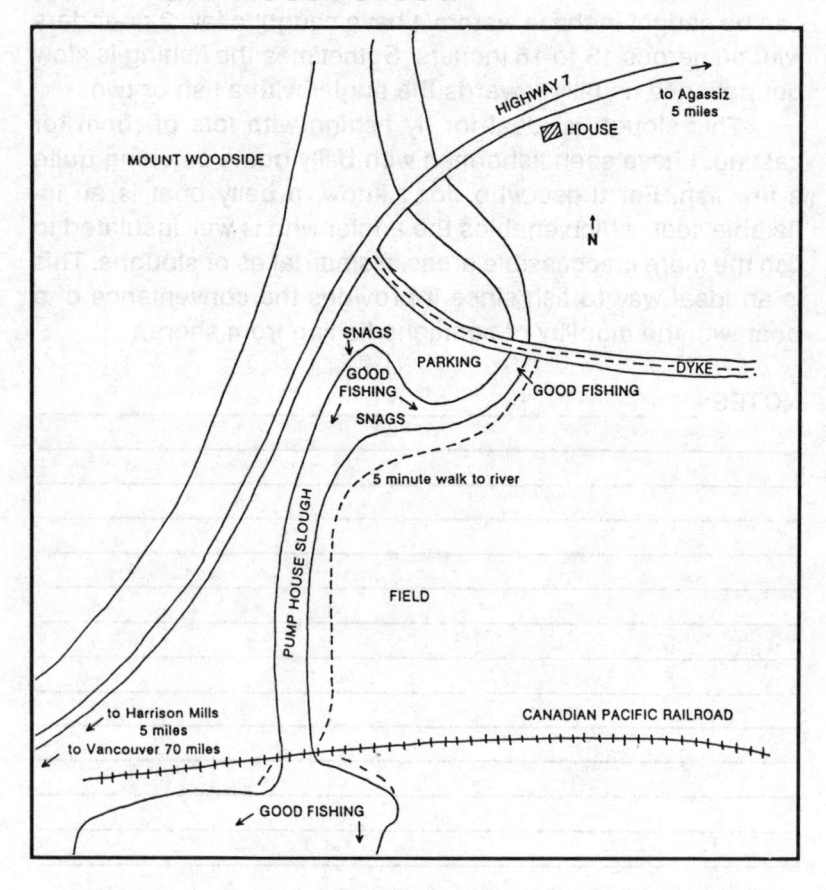

A word of warning: the Pump House Slough has numerous snags especially in the wider bay by the parking lot. If you bottom fish be prepared to lose gear. It might be wiser to fish with a float and worm or with flies. Last December, I watched a seasoned fly fisherman catch and release fish after fish using a special hand-tied fly, which he kept a secret. If you catch a run going through, the fly fishing can be quite good.

If you want to fish the mouth of this slough where it enters the Fraser River, you must cross a field, which is private property. Please treat this land with respect, since you are a guest. Incidently, the mouth of the slough can be very good fishing.

This little slough doesn't get much attention but it is countless little waters like this that are the backbone of the cutthroat populations. Many of these little waters have disappeared with the onslaught of civilization. However, without these streams and sloughs, the cutthroat trout populations would be much reduced.

The Pump House Slough is accessible and easily fished from shore. Perhaps you won't catch trophy-sized fish here but you can usually be sure of a trout or two.

NOTES: _____

8 TRANMER'S BAR

Tranmer's Bar is 2.4 kilometers or 1.5 miles east of Agassiz. It has been an excellent spot over the years, with good catches of cutthroat trout, coho, whitefish and the odd Dolly Varden, steelhead and spring salmon.

To get to Tranmer's Bar, follow the same directions as for the mouth of Maria Slough. Parking along the road is advisable, especially if you don't have a truck.

This bar has changed considerably in the last nine years but it is still good fishing. My notes indicate that 1986, in

MAP 12 TRANMER'S BAR

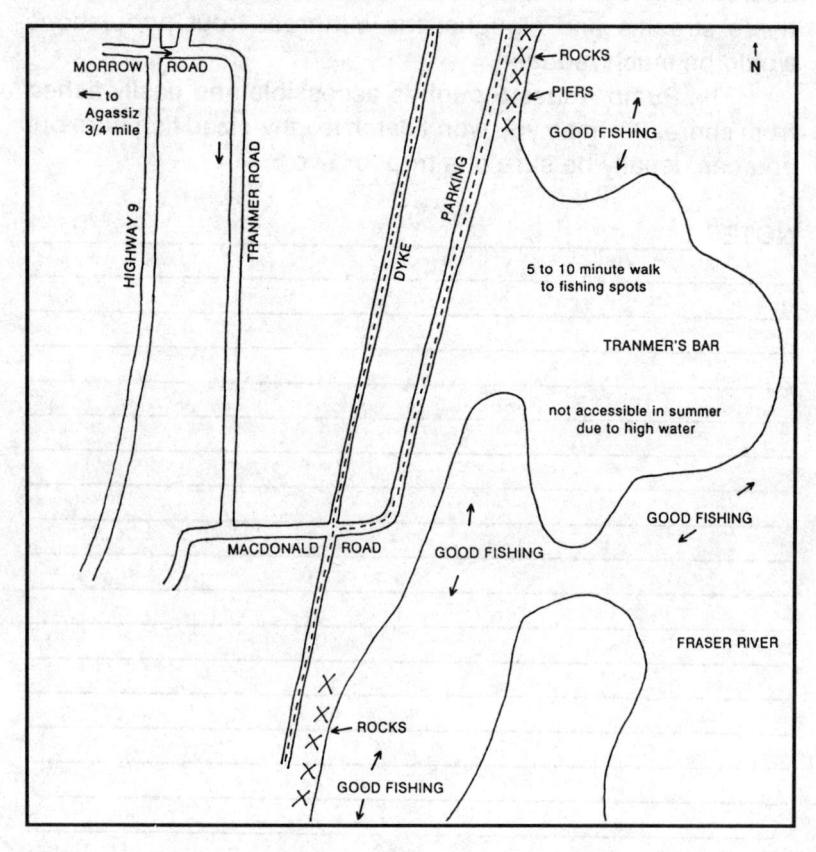

particular, was a very good year with eight cutthroat trout over 2 pounds. These fish were all caught in the last week of October and the first week of November. Large cutthroat trout can be finicky biters and all these fish nibbled at my worm. I had to react quickly to very small nibbles. Sometimes, too, cutthroat trout will play with the worm, bringing in the line and making it difficult to set the hook. Occasionally cutthroat will hit-and-run but this is more characteristic of rainbows and salmon. Cutthroat trout are usually persistent which makes them easier to catch than the wily rainbows.

As for Tranmer's Bar itself, there are plenty of good fishing spots. Try fishing upstream from the piers along the northern part of the bar. The coho and cutthroat trout tend to swim near the shore, on their way to Maria Slough. When the coho run starts in the middle of October or beginning of November, fishing can be good. Most fishermen use a salmon rod and reel, 12 to 15 pound test line and use salmon roe, wool or lures.

Downstream from the piers can be good fishing, as is the little bay in the southwestern portion of the bar. The latter is where I caught all my fish in 1986. It's also where I caught my biggest cutthroat trout, a 3-pound 20-inch beauty. Fishing is also good along the western side by the rocks. In 1987, I caught numerous 1 1/2- to 2-pound trout in this spot. In October, before the November rains, the channel dissecting Tranmer's Bar is often dry, enabling fishermen to walk and fish further up the bar. Fishing here can be quite good too.

Almost anything will work on Tranmer's Bar—worms, eggs, roe, wool, lures and flies. October and November are the best months with a few trout in February and March.

NOTES _____

9 MORROW'S BAR

This bar is located 3.2 kilometers or 2 miles southeast of Agassiz, near the Agassiz-Rosedale Bridge. It has coho and steelhead in the fall and cutthroat trout in the fall, winter and spring.

To get to Morrow's Bar turn right on Macdonald Road, which is the second right-hand turnoff past the Agassiz-Rosedale Bridge. Shortly after turning right there is a fork in the road; take the left fork, which is still Macdonald Road. Go

MAP 13 MORROW'S BAR

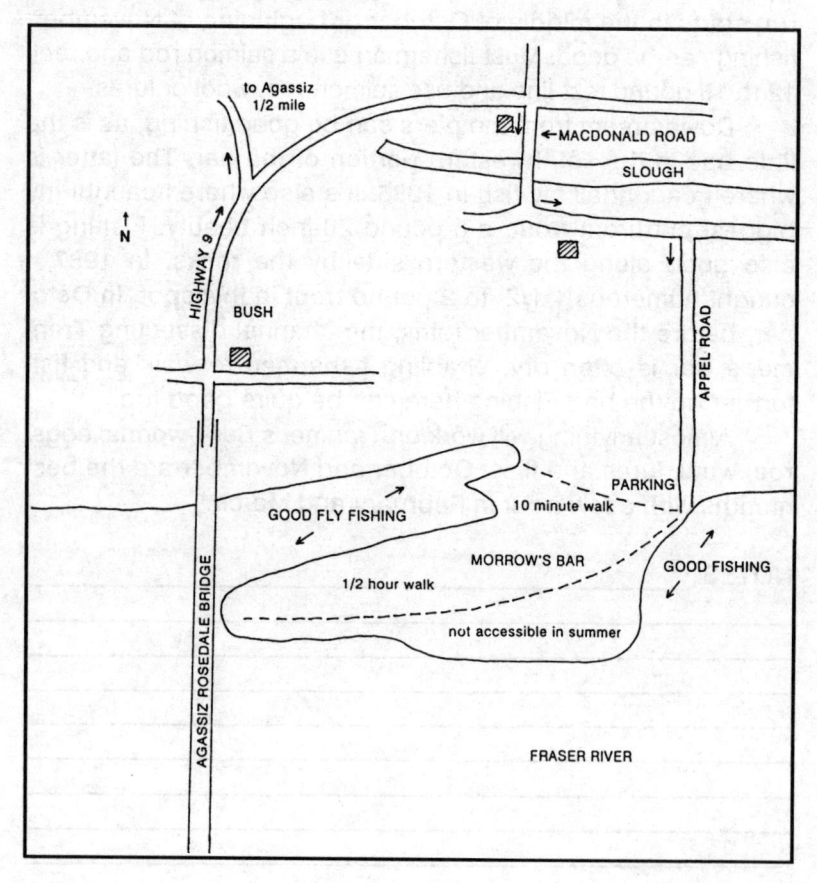

along Macdonald Road then turn right at Appel Road and go down its entire length over the dyke to a parking spot near the Fraser River. Some people take their trucks to the end of the bar or go over to the head of the backwater under the Agassiz-Rosedale Bridge. It will take you half an hour to walk to the end of Morrow's Bar and about ten minutes to walk to the end of the backwater under the Agassiz-Rosedale Bridge.

Along the Fraser shore there is good fishing for coho and steelhead in September and October. Some people fish the end of Morrow's Bar, which in low water extends under the Agassiz-Rosedale Bridge. For bar fishing, a long casting rod is recommended with at least 12 pound test line.

The slough under the Agassiz-Rosedale Bridge, on the Morrow's Bar side is a good place for fly fishing. Try a belly boat or chest waders. Morrow's Bar is not fished as heavily as Tranmer's Bar but the fishing can, at times, be just as good. One day in September, 1991 was particularly memorable. In a 3 hour period, I hooked and released about a dozen pink salmon. I also caught two coho, one 8 pounds the other 5 pounds. In addition, I hooked a spring salmon of approximately 15 pounds, only to have the hook break off, leaving the fish free to swim away! Morrow's Bar can supply some fine fishing on occasions.

NOTES: _____
_____
_____
_____
_____
_____
_____
_____
_____
_____
_____
_____
_____
_____
_____
_____

10 MIAMI RIVER

This river runs through Harrison Hot Springs. It has some occasionally good catches of cutthroat trout, rainbows, Dolly Varden and coho. The mouth of the river, where it empties into Harrison Lake near the Harrison Hotel, is perhaps the best place to fish.

In summer, rainbows are caught near the mouth of the river, sometimes of good size. In the fall, after the November rains, the mouth is a good spot for cutthroat trout and coho. Salmon roe, worms and lures are all effective.

Some people fish further up the river in the fall for coho and cutthroat trout.

NOTES: _____
_____
_____
_____

MAP 14 MIAMI RIVER

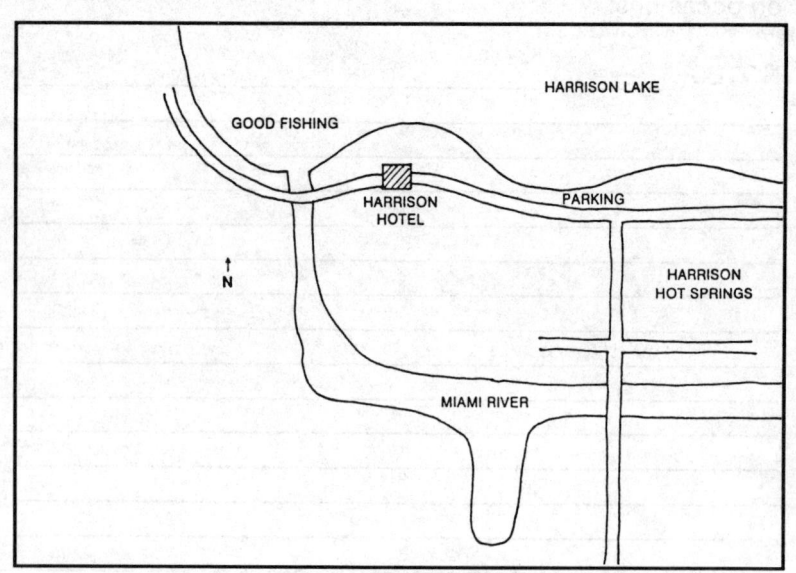

11   BOUCHARD'S SLOUGH

This slough is south of Agassiz, just over the dyke. It has some good catches of cutthroat trout with a few coho in the fall. To get to this spot take the Highway 401 turnoff into Agassiz, crossing the Agassiz-Rosedale Bridge. Turn left on Whelpton Road the first road past the bridge. This is a very sharp turn so be alert. Follow this road to the end and turn left on Tuyttens Road, continue over the dyke past a large house on the right. Take the first right turn on this gravel road and proceed until you arrive at the parking area on the right. Park here.

Thirty years ago Bouchard's Slough was a real hot spot, with excellent catches of cutthroat trout, coho and even the odd steelhead. For various reasons, the slough declined to the point where it was nicknamed "Sucker Slough." However, the slough is slowly recovering, with increasing numbers of cut-

MAP 15   BOUCHARD'S SLOUGH

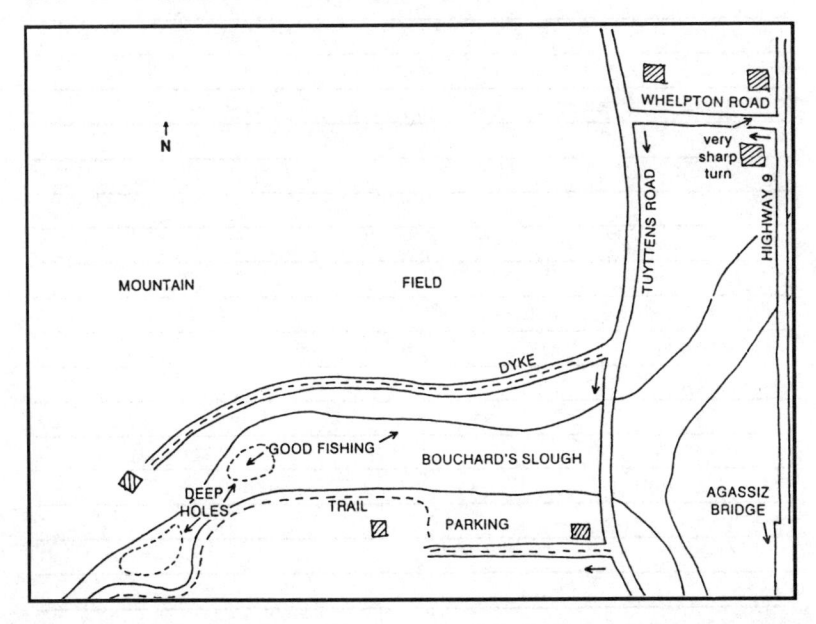

throat trout. This year, I caught and released numerous trout, including one 16-inch 1 1/2-pound cutthroat.

NOTES:

OTHER AREAS

I have fished all of these spots at least once. They are less known to me but are still popular areas.

12) HOPE RIVER
Hope River is 4 kilometers or 2.5 miles northeast of Chilliwack and is 13 kilometers or 8.1 miles in length. It has cutthroat trout and a few coho in the fall. Access is via municipal roads and private property.

13) KAWKAWA LAKE
Kawkawa Lake is a popular fishing spot 2 kilometers or 1.2 miles east of Hope. The lake is 77 hectares or 190 acres in area and contains cutthroat trout, Dolly Varden char, kokanee (landlocked sockeye salmon), coho juveniles and some non-salmonid species. This is an excellent lake for kokanee with catches of 2 pounds or more common. A park with a boat launch is present.

14) SILVER LAKE
Silver Lake is 12 kilometers or 7.5 miles south of the junction of Highway 1 and the Silver Skagit Road. The lake is 40 hectares or 98.8 acres in size and contains kokanee, steelhead and Dolly Varden char. The kokanee tend to be small but the Dolly Varden char may reach 2 kilos or 5 pounds.

15) LAKE OF THE WOODS
Lake of the Woods is beside Highway 1, 4 kilometers or 2.5 miles north of Hope. The lake is 17 hectares or 42 acres in area and is stocked with rainbows, providing good catches to 35 centimeters or 14 inches. A private resort and boat launch is on the lake.

NOTES: _____
_____
_____

II FOR THE KNOWLEDGEABLE AND EXPERIENCED

"The barriers between fish and fishermen are many and significant."
—Roderick Haig Brown
Fisherman's Fall

16 THE BEAVER POND

Over the years, this little 5-acre pond near Hicks Lake in Sasquatch Park has produced many a fine catch. There are some big fish in here, both rainbow and cutthroat trout. Try the west side in the spring and the east side in the summer and fall, during low water. Worms work well here as do single eggs and flies. This pond is ideal for a belly boat or chest waders. A nature trail goes around the pond, opening the entire area for fishing.

MAP 16 THE BEAVER POND

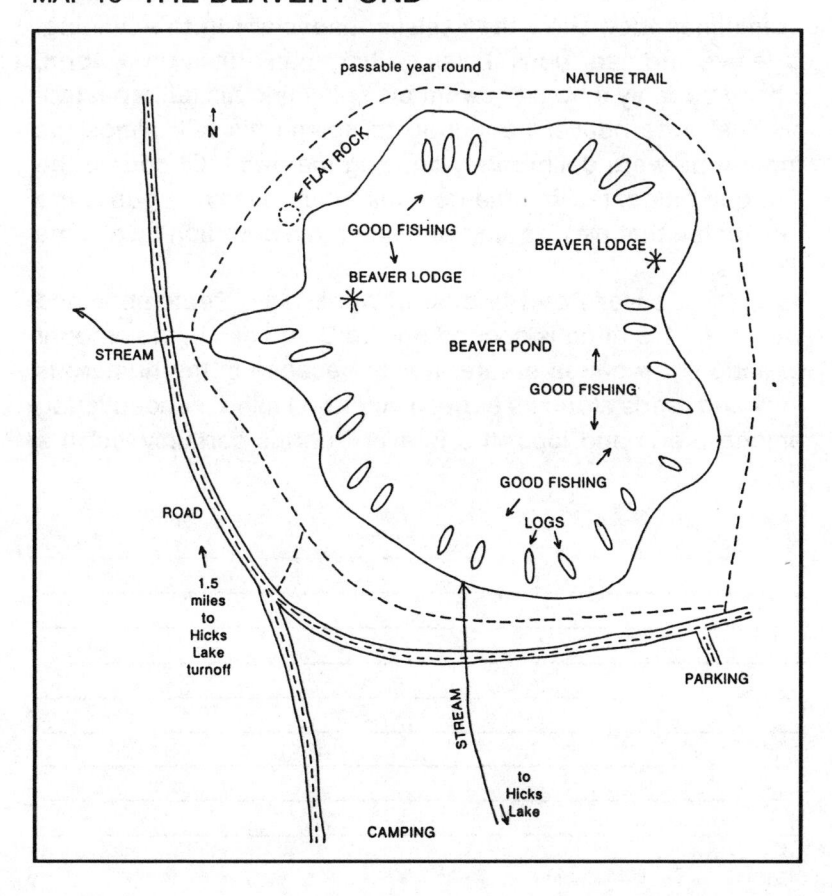

My most memorable fish from the Beaver Pond was an acrobatic 14-inch rainbow trout, caught in early May 1985. This was a slow day for the Beaver Pond, with only one small trout to show for my day's effort. I was thinking of returning home when suddenly my rod bent in half and the reel screeched as the trout grabbed my worm and ran. That fish jumped six times before finally giving up. Acrobatics like this are common with rainbow trout.

Another memorable day was when I hooked a large trout, only to have it get hung up on the reeds. Undaunted, I took off my boots and pants and waded into the water to free my fish. I managed to free the fish from the reeds but the struggle loosened the hook leaving the fish free to swim away.

There are two lodges in this pond, with several beavers. Sometimes they show themselves, especially in the evening. One evening near dusk, I was getting many bites on a worm, when suddenly a beaver swam by, splashing his tail repeatedly. That irate beaver continued to splash his tail, almost as though he were deliberately chasing me away. Of course the fish quit biting, leaving me no choice but to leave. I guess the beaver felt that he was king of his domain and didn't welcome visitors.

The Beaver Pond is best in April, May, September and October. This pond is second only to Deer Lake in the amount of action. It requires greater ability because of the numerous logs and reeds along its edge. If you don't mind manoeuvering among reeds and logs, the Beaver Pond is certainly worth a try.

NOTES: _____
_____
_____
_____
_____
_____
_____
_____

17 WEAVER LAKE

At one time in the 1960s, Weaver Lake was perhaps the best trout lake in the Fraser Valley. Today it is still a popular lake with good catches of rainbow trout. The lake is 14 kilometers or 8.4 miles northeast of Harrison Mills, with access via Morris Valley Road and a logging road. The lake is 81 hectares or 200 acres in area and is stocked with rainbow trout, which produce catches to 40 centimeters or 16 inches. This is a fly fishing lake. Try trolling flies or a wedding band lure and worm. This lake is best in May, June, September and October. Do not leave vehicle at road.

NOTES: _____
_____
_____
_____

MAP 17 WEAVER LAKE

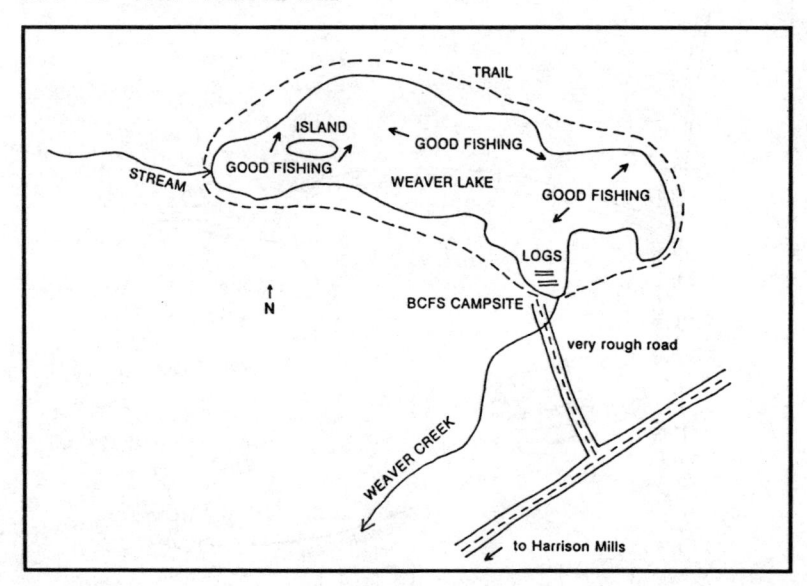

18 MORRIS LAKE

Morris Lake is 8 hectares or 20 acres in size and is 11 kilometers or 6.8 miles northeast of Harrison Mills. Access is via Morris Valley Road and a secondary logging road. The final 300 yards are rough and steep so I recommend parking your vehicle by the road and walking to the lake. A truck is recommended. The lake has cutthroat trout to 20 inches or 50 centimeters and whitefish. Try worms, roe, and flies for best results. Check the regulations closely for special rules.

NOTES: _____
_____
_____
_____
_____
_____

MAP 18 **MORRIS LAKE**

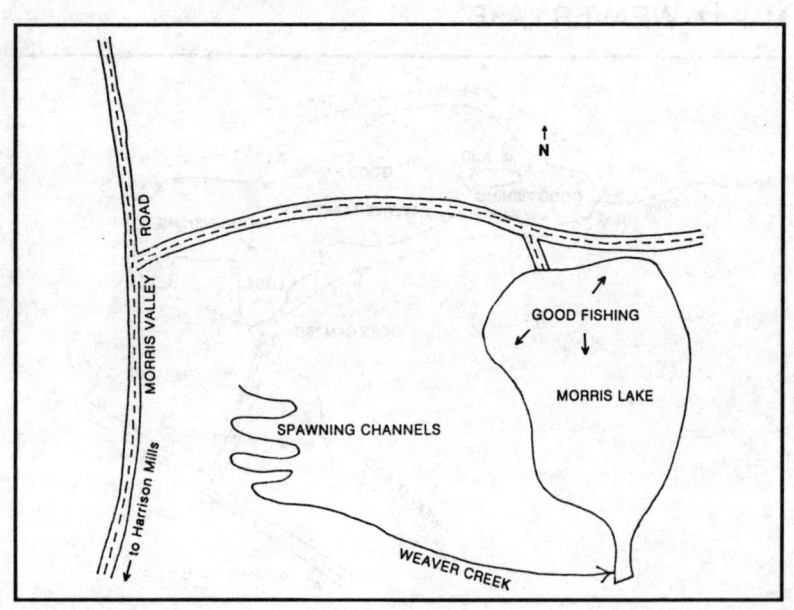

19 HARRISON RIVER

Sixty to eighty years ago the Harrison River was world renowned for its fine cutthroat trout fishing. People came from all over North America and Europe to fish these waters. Then for some reason, perhaps logging, perhaps disease, the cutthroat population crashed. Today, with the salmonid enhancement program, the cutthroat trout is making a comeback in the Harrison River. Who knows, in another ten years, the Harrison may once again be a premier trout stream.

MAP 19 HARRISON RIVER SHOWING BOAT LAUNCH

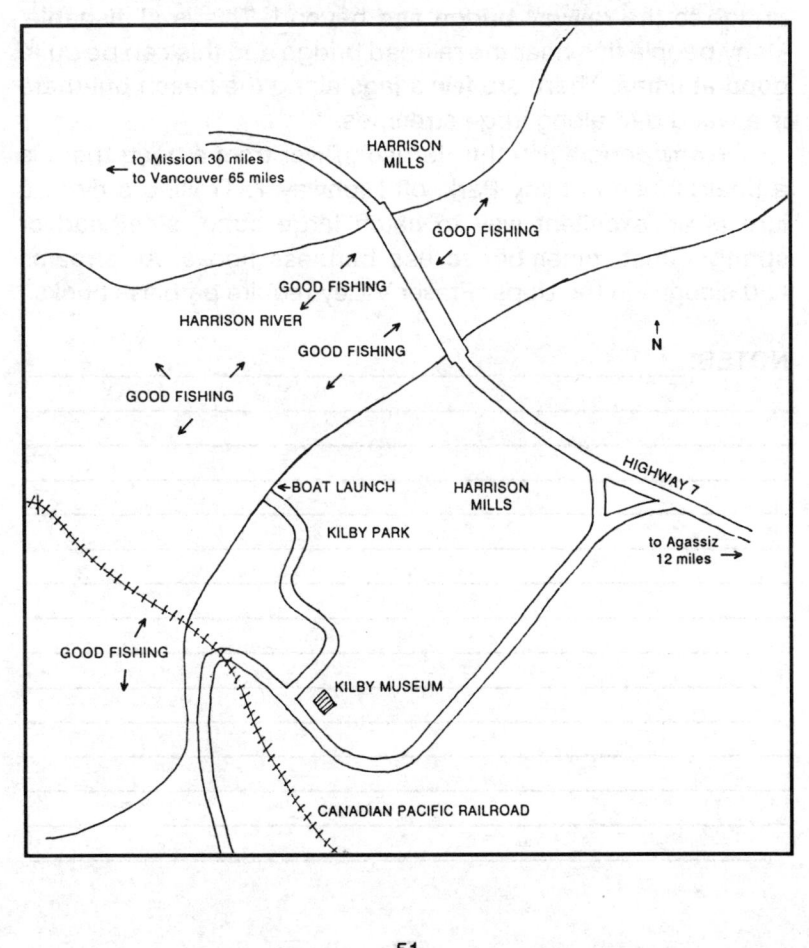

The Harrison River is a large stream running from Harrison Lake to the Fraser River, with 13 kilometers or 8 miles of fishable length. The Harrison has good runs of cutthroat trout, steelhead, coho, springs, whitefish and Dolly Varden char.

The river is good for cutthroat from April through to December. Coho are caught in October and November, while steelhead are caught in December and January. Try worms, roe, eggs, lures and flies for cutthroat trout and roe, wool or lures for coho and steelhead. Many people driftfish with roe or wool using a salmon rod and reel, a float and 12 pound test line.

One of the best places to fish is upstream from the road bridge at Harrison Mills, wearing chestwaders and casting lures or flies. There is also a large beach area from the road bridge to the railway bridge and beyond. This is all fishable. Many people fish near the railroad bridge and this can be quite good at times. There are few snags along the beach but there is a weed bed along large stretches.

Many people fish the Harrison River from a boat; there is a boat launch in Kilby Park, off Highway 7. Trolling a fly or a lure is an excellent way to catch large coho, steelhead or springs. Just remember to use barbless hooks. All streams and sloughs in the Upper Fraser Valley require barbless hooks.

NOTES: _____
_____
_____
_____
_____
_____
_____
_____
_____
_____
_____
_____
_____
_____

SMALL LOWER LEVEL LAKES

I have fished these areas once or twice. They provide good catches of rainbow trout but a truck is recommended.

20 ELBOW LAKE

Elbow Lake is 14 hectares or 35 acres in size. It is regularly stocked with rainbows, providing good catches of small fish. Access is via a logging road north from Harrison Mills.

21 GRACE LAKE

Grace Lake is a 6-hectare or 16-acre pond 12 kilometers or 7.5 miles northeast of Harrison Mills. Access is via Morris Valley Road and Harrison West Logging Road. The lake has rainbows to 30 to 35 centimeters or 12 to 14 inches. A British Columbia Forest Service campsite is nearby; no power boats are allowed.

22 FRANCIS LAKE

This 4-hectare or 10-acre pond is 18 kilometers or 11.2 miles northeast of Harrison Mills via Morris Valley Road and Harrison West Logging Road. The lake has small rainbows. A British Columbia Forest Service campsite is present; no power boats are allowed.

23 WOLF LAKE

This tiny pond is only 2 hectares or 5 acres in size and is located just north of Grace Lake. It has rainbows, with catches similar to those from Grace Lake. A British Columbia Forest Service campsite is present; no power boats are allowed.

24 WOOD LAKE

Wood Lake is 5 hectares or 12 acres in area and is located 30 kilometers or 18.6 miles northeast of Harrison Mills. Access is via Morris Valley Road and Harrison West Logging Road. The lake has rainbows to 30 centimeters or 12 inches. A British Columbia Forest Campsite is nearby; no power boats are allowed.

25 FOLEY LAKE

Foley Lake is 40 kilometers or 24.9 miles southeast of Chilliwack. Access is via the Chilliwack Lake Road and a secondary road. The lake has rainbows and Dolly Varden char to 35 centimeters or 14 inches. A British Columbia Forest Service campsite is present.

NOTES:

26 TUNNELS BAR

This bar is not fished as much as the other bars in Agassiz, but it still produces good catches of trout, whitefish and coho salmon. The bar is located at the base of Mount Woodside, just past the Canadian Pacific Railway tunnels. Take care while going through the tunnels; listen for the whistle blasts that warn of an oncoming train. Be sure to wear hip waders, since you usually have to wade through water to get out to the bar. For best results try worms, roe or lures.

NOTES: _____
_____
_____

MAP 20 TUNNELS BAR

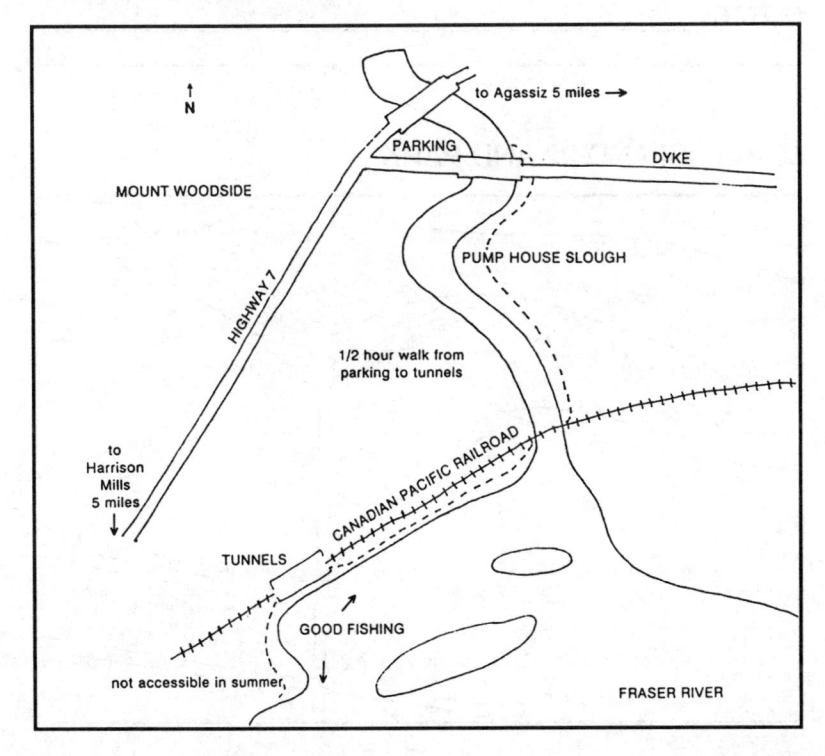

27 ISLAND 22 AND PARK

Island 22 is near Chilliwack. I have included a diagram because of its popularity. Sometimes the fishing here is very good. Most people use large heavy casting rods and reels with a spin and glow lure and several ounces of weight. Simply cast the lure and weight as far out as possible and wait for a fish to strike. This is a good spot for coho, springs, steelhead and large cutthroat trout. A boat launch is available at Island 22 Park for access to Severn Islands in the Fraser River.

To get to Island 22 Park, drive through Chilliwack along Yale Road until you come to Menzies Street, where you turn left. A Shop Easy store marks the street. Turn left onto Hope River Road, then turn right onto Young Road and left onto Cartmell Street, which will take you to Island 22 Park.

NOTES: _____

_____

MAP 21 ISLAND 22 AND PARK

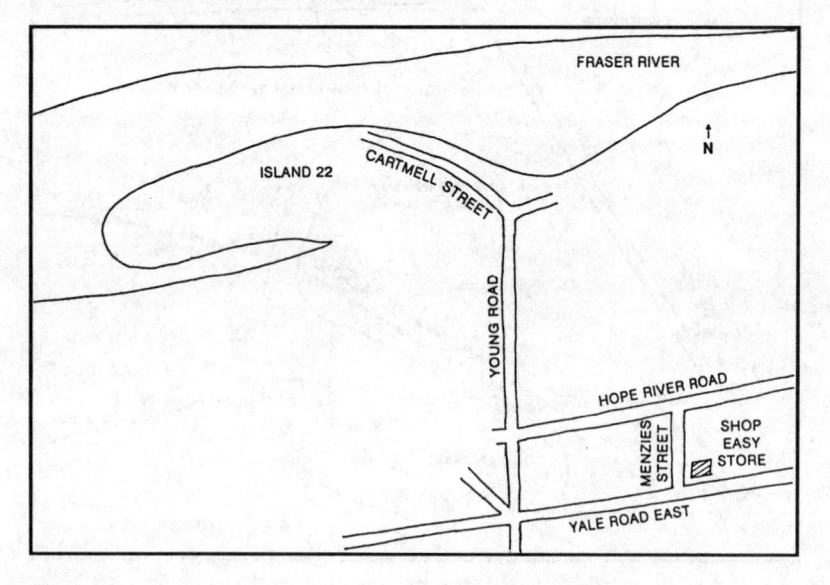

28 LINDEMAN AND GREENDROP LAKES

Lindeman Lake is 12 hectares or 30 acres in area and is located along the Centennial Trail 50 kilometers or 31.2 miles southeast of Chilliwack, with access via the Chilliwack Lake Road and Post Creek. The lake has rainbows to 35 centimeters or 14 inches. A short hike of 2 kilometers or 1.2 miles is required for Lindeman Lake while Greendrop Lake is 6 kilometers or 3.7 miles from Post Creek. Greendrop Lake is 21 hectares or 52 acres in area and has excellent fly fishing for rainbows to 45 centimeters or 18 inches. There is a British Columbia Forest Service campsite at Post Creek. For these higher altitude lakes, I recommend a folding rod to make backpacking easier. Flies can be fished with a plastic bubble, thus eliminating the need for a fly fishing rod. Single eggs work well here as do worms. But with such excellent fly fishing, why use natural baits?

MAP 22 LINDEMAN AND GREENDROP LAKES

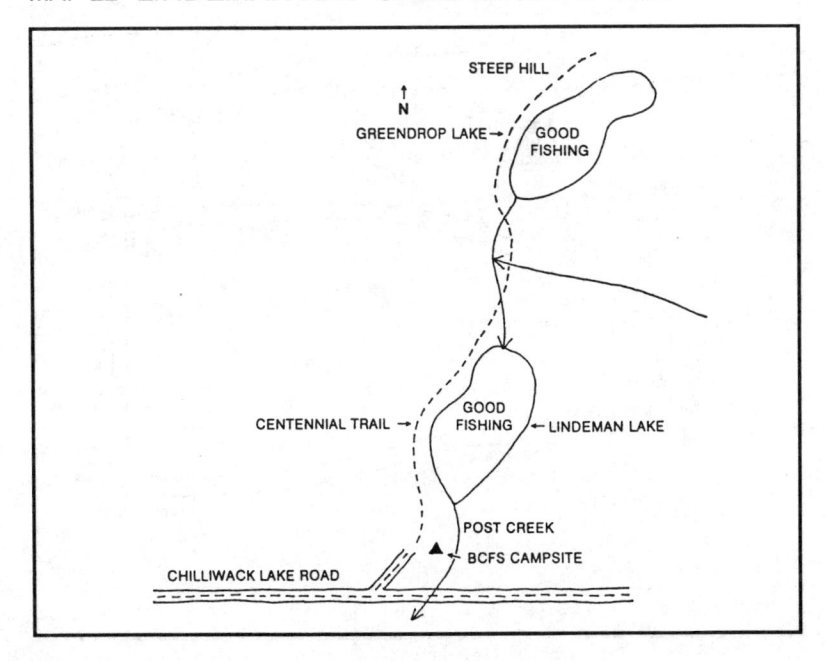

29 OTHER CHILLIWACK AREA BARS

The Chilliwack-Rosedale area contains numerous bars. Try at the ends of McSween and Jesperson roads in Chilliwack, and at the ends of Gill and McGrath roads in Rosedale and past the reserve in Popkum. These bars produce cutthroat trout to 2 pounds or more, coho to 15 pounds as well as springs, steelhead, whitefish and the odd Dolly Varden. I don't know this area very well but have included a diagram since many people may want to fish closer to Chilliwack.

NOTES: _____
_____
_____
_____

MAP 23 OTHER CHILLIWACK AREA BARS

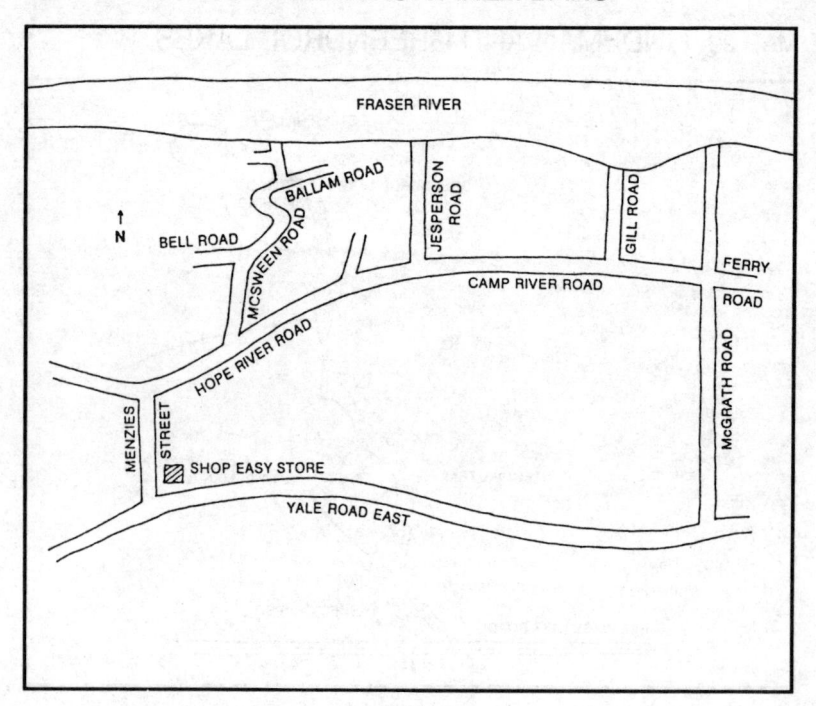

30 THE VEDDER-CHILLIWACK RIVER

This medium-sized stream is 7 kilometers or 4.4 miles south of Chilliwack. It is known as the Chilliwack River above the Vedder Bridge and the Vedder River below the Vedder Bridge. Fishable length is 36 kilometers or 22.4 miles to Slesse Creek. Access is via numerous municipal roads in the Vedder area and the Chilliwack Lake Road above the bridge. British Columbia Forest Service campsites are scattered along the river.

MAP 24 THE VEDDER-CHILLIWACK RIVER

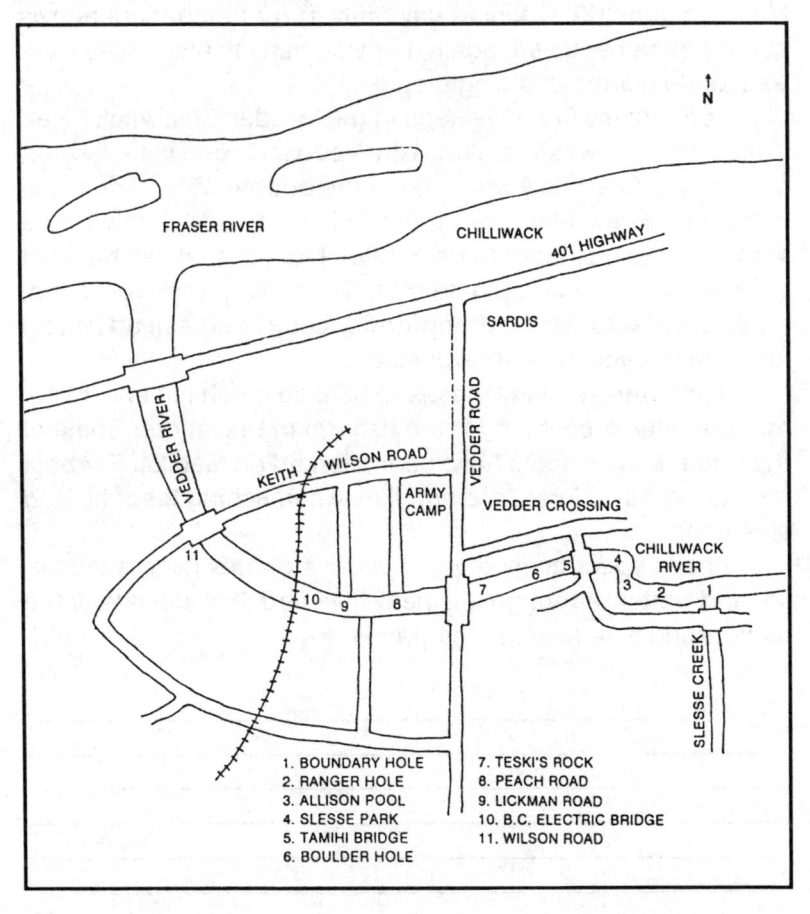

1. BOUNDARY HOLE
2. RANGER HOLE
3. ALLISON POOL
4. SLESSE PARK
5. TAMIHI BRIDGE
6. BOULDER HOLE
7. TESKI'S ROCK
8. PEACH ROAD
9. LICKMAN ROAD
10. B.C. ELECTRIC BRIDGE
11. WILSON ROAD

This is a very popular and crowded river, with numerous bars, whorls, back eddies, currents and pockets along its fishable length. In the fall and winter, it is advisable to fish as early as possible if you want a good spot.

The Vedder-Chilliwack River has an excellent run of winter steelhead—December through March are the best months. The river also has an excellent run of coho, which starts at the end of September and runs to the beginning of November. In the summer, large numbers of hatchery rainbows are released from the hatchery above Slesse Creek, providing good sport in July and August. The river also has cutthroat trout, spring salmon, white fish and Dolly Varden char.

The Vedder-Chilliwack River is closed for fishing from May 1 to June 30. Opening day (July 1) for hatchery rainbows can be quite hectic so, again, I advise early fishing. Flies work well as do worms and single eggs.

I caught my first steelhead in the Vedder-Chilliwack River. I was fishing downstream from the Vedder Bridge in fast water, bouncing a fresh dew worm along the bottom. When the steelhead hit, I knew that I had a fight on my hands. I only had a small trout rod so I had to be careful. I fought that fish for what seemed like an eternity before finally landing, then releasing, a wild steelhead. That was my introduction to steelhead fishing and I have been hooked ever since.

There are so many places to fish, so much fishable water that the river is best left for the fisherman to explore. Some of the better known spots have been marked on Map 24. For best results, try yarn, lures, roe and flies when fishing for coho and steelhead.

I have spent many enjoyable days on this river, summer, fall and winter. Although it is heavily fished, it is still one of the most productive rivers in the province.

NOTES:_____
_____
_____
_____
_____
_____

31 UNDER AGASSIZ BRIDGE ON THE ROSEDALE SIDE

Twenty years ago this was a real hot spot, with good catches of coho, springs and steelhead. This spot is ideal for heavy bar fishing with a hefty rod, sturdy reel, heavy line and sinkers. Personally, I don't like heavy gear but don't let my biases prevent you from trying this spot, for it can still be good fishing at times. Try in the fall for coho and steelhead and in August for springs.

NOTES: _____
_____

MAP 25 UNDER AGASSIZ BRIDGE ON ROSEDALE SIDE

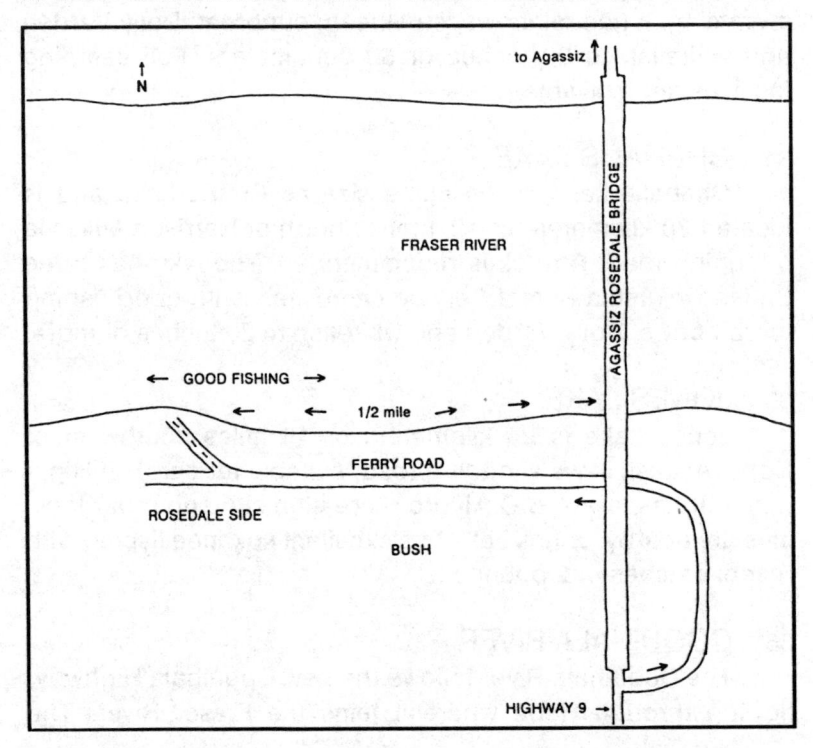

OTHER AREAS

I have fished all of these spots except Jones Lake; for Jones Lake I have relied on my fishing contacts for general information.

32   CHILLIWACK LAKE
This large lake is 1,198 hectares or 2,969 acres in area and is 48 kilometers or 29.8 miles southeast of Chilliwack via a gravel road. The lake contains rainbow and cutthroat trout to 35 centimeters and Dolly Varden char to 2 kilos or 5 pounds. Full camping facilities are present.

33   CULTUS LAKE
Cultus Lake is 13 kilometers or 8 miles south of Chilliwack on a paved road. The lake is 628 hectares or 1,552 acres in size and is heavily used for fishing, boating, water skiing and swimming. It has rainbows, steelhead, cutthroat, Dolly Varden and whitefish to 20 inches or 50 centimeters. Full camping facilities are available.

34   CHEHALIS LAKE
Chehalis Lake is the same size as Cultus Lake and is located 20 kilometers or 12.4 miles north of Harrison Mills via a logging road. A truck is recommended. The lake has three British Columbia Forest Service campsites, with good fishing for rainbows, Dolly Varden and whitefish to 20 inches or more.

35   JONES LAKE
Jones Lake is 24 kilometers or 15 miles southwest of Hope. Access is via a logging road, suitable for cars, off Highway 1 at Laidlaw. A B.C. Hydro recreation site and other facilities are nearby. Jones Lake has excellent kokanee fishing with recent catches of 2 pounds.

36   COQUIHALA RIVER
The Coquihala River follows the new Coquihala Highway, flowing through Hope where it joins the Fraser River. The

Coquihala River has fair runs of summer and winter steelhead plus Dolly Varden and a few coho. Check the regulations carefully, since this is a closely-monitored stream.

NOTES: _____

III FOR THE DEDICATED AND SKILLED

"Is it not an art to deceive a trout with an artificial fly?"

—Izaak Walton
The Complete Angler (1653)

37 THE CHEHALIS RIVER

The Chehalis River flows from Chehalis Lake to the Harrison River, with a fishable length of 18 kilometers or 11 miles. Access is via Morris Valley Road northeast of Harrison Mills. The Chehalis has a small run of summer steelhead, a larger run of winter steelhead, a large run of coho in October, November and December. The river also has Dolly Varden char, cutthroat trout and whitefish.

Most people driftfish with roe or use lures, wool, and flies. The Chehalis can often be crowded so early fishing is advisable. The best areas are the Chehalis Canyon, behind the fish hatchery, and downstream from the old Pretty homestead. As a cautionary note, it is advisable to keep any valuables out of sight to eliminate possible theft. The Chehalis River is subject to sudden high water after rains and the canyon trail is difficult and treacherous, so be careful.

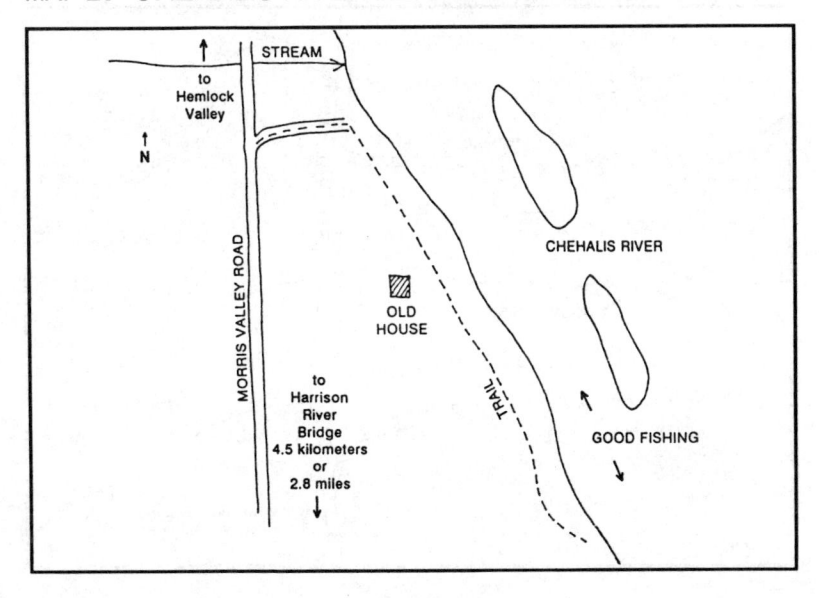

MAP 26 CHEHALIS RIVER BEHIND PRETTY HOMESTEAD

MAP 27 CHEHALIS RIVER BEHIND FISH HATCHERY

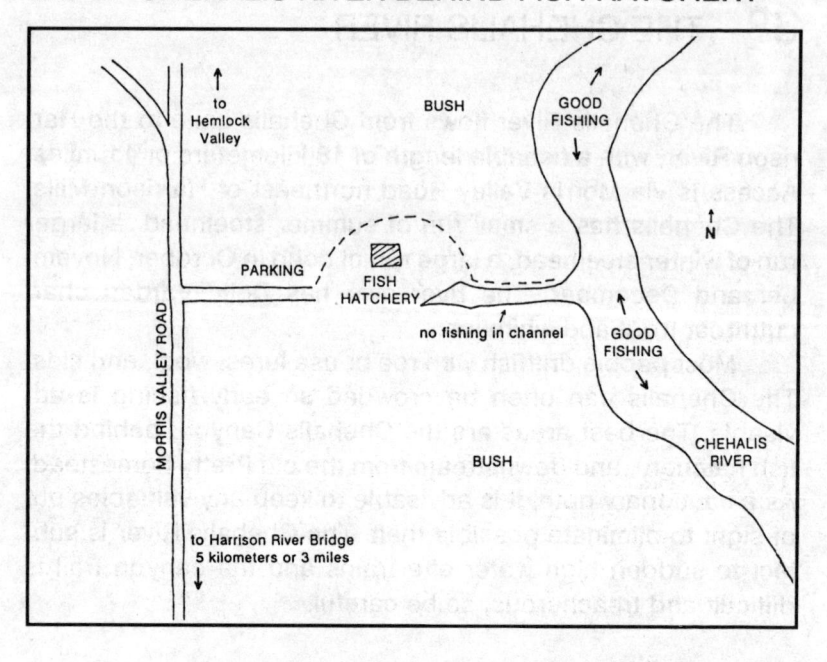

MAP 28 CHEHALIS RIVER CANYON AND BRIDGE AREA

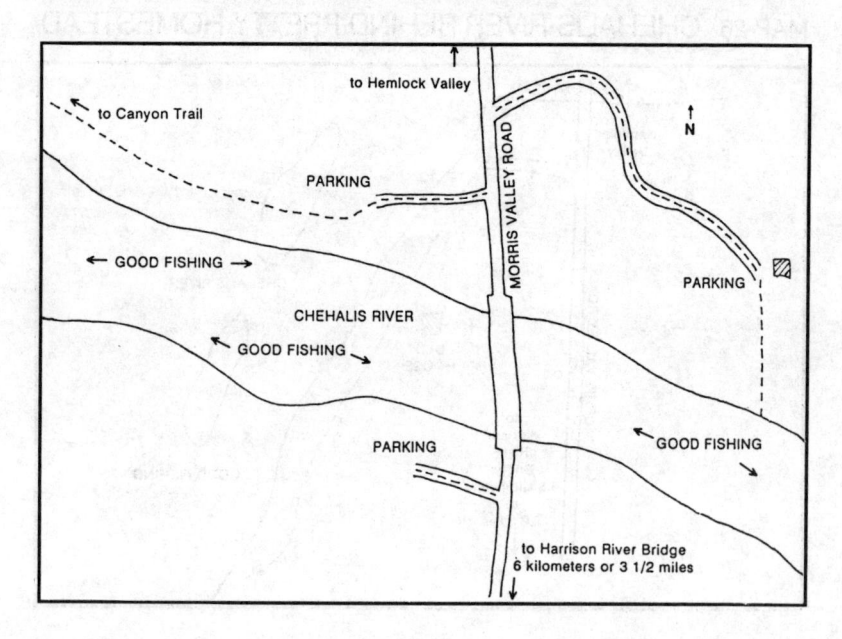

38 HARRISON LAKE

Harrison Lake is the largest lake in the region. It is 21,780 hectares or 53,810 acres in area and over 64 kilometers or 40 miles in length. The lake contains cutthroat trout to 40 centimeters or 16 inches, rainbow trout to 1.5 kilos or 4 pounds, whitefish, sturgeon, and numerous nonsalmonid species. Full camping facilities, lodging and a boat launching area are available in Harrison Hot Springs. This is a volatile lake with sudden wind shifts and squalls, so be careful. The lake is best fished in the numerous bays and coves. The mouth of the Harrison River is sometimes good, as is Cascade Bay.

NOTES: _____
_____
_____

MAP 29 HARRISON LAKE SOUTH

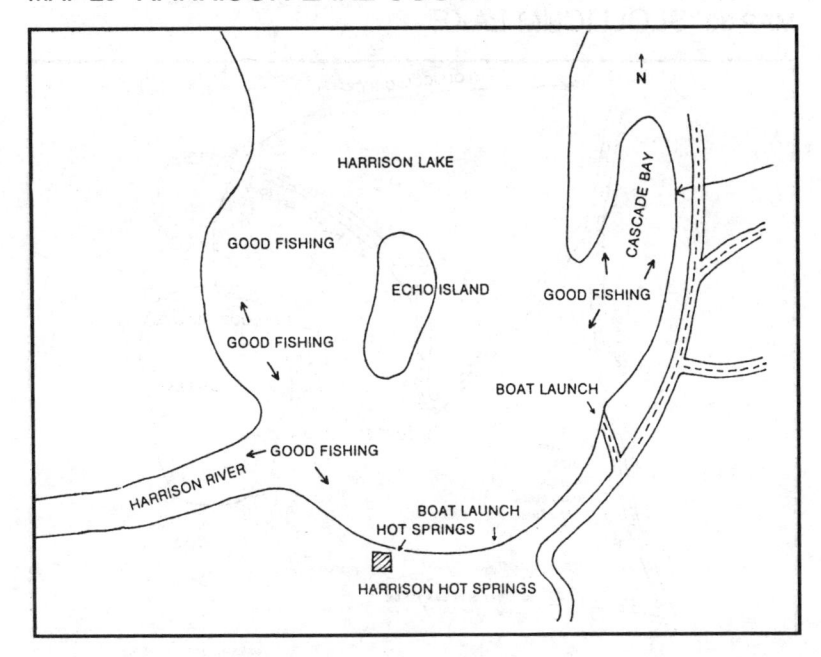

39 SLOLLICUM LAKE

This small 26-hectare or 65-acre alpine lake is 16 kilometers or 10 miles northeast of Harrison Hot Springs. Access is via Sasquatch Park, Harrison East Logging Road, a secondary road and a final hike of 3 kilometers or 1.9 miles. A truck is definitely needed, preferably with four-wheel-drive. As for fishing, try the bluffs near the trail's end—look down and see the rainbow trout swimming. The fish here tend to be small but they are plentiful and readily taken on a fly. Worms or single eggs also work well.

NOTES: _____
_____
_____
_____
_____

MAP 30 SLOLLICUM LAKE

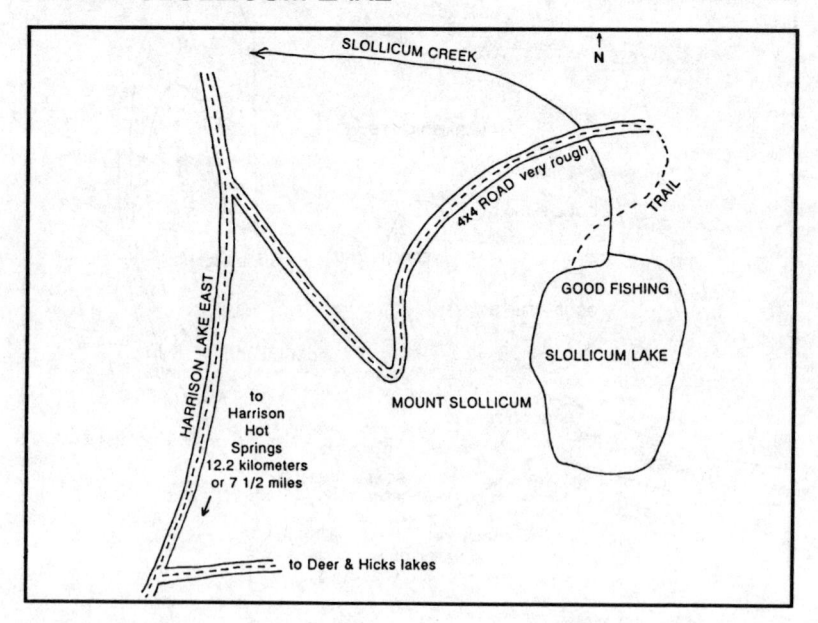

40 STATLU LAKE

This alpine lake is located a few miles past Chehalis Lake via a good logging road that is open weekends only. A short half hour walk takes you into the lake but you can walk along the lake for another half to three-quarters of an hour. It is stocked with rainbows which tend to be small. The setting here is very picturesque, much like the Rocky Mountains. This is a good spot for a combined fishing—picnic expedition. If the fish don't bite, you can always enjoy a good meal and some fine scenery.

NOTES: _____
_____
_____
_____

Map 31 STATLU LAKE

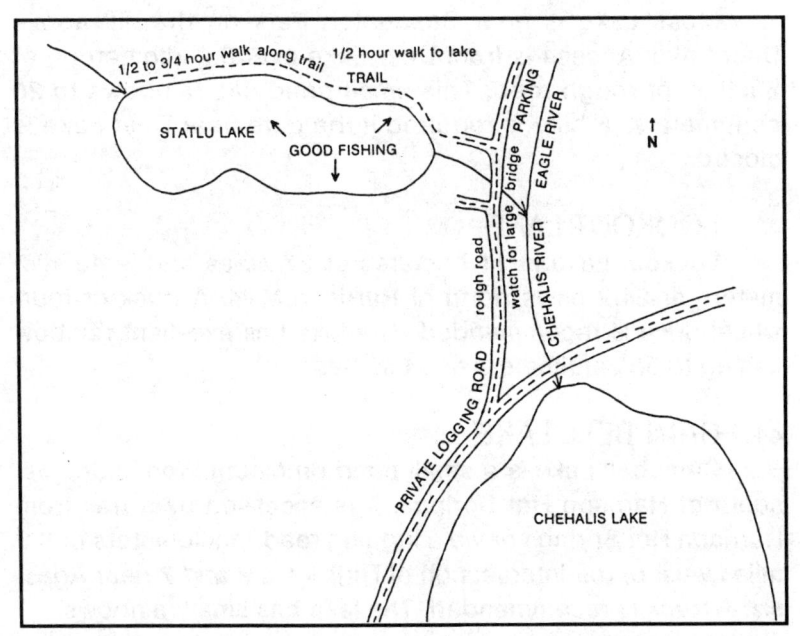

OTHER AREAS

I have fished all of these areas except Hanging Lake, Pierce Lake, Flora Lake and Wilson Lake. For these lakes, I have relied on my fishing contacts.

Hardly anyone fishes these spots but don't let that deter you for the fishing can be fantastic. Most of these spots require a stiff hike while some of them need an overnight stay. This, of course, deters most fishermen, but there are always a few hardy souls willing to work hard to get away from everything and fish in a wilderness or semiwilderness setting. If you are one of those hardy souls read on!

41 WEAVER CREEK

This stream flows from Weaver Lake to Morris Lake with only 2 kilometers or 1.2 miles of fishable length. The creek contains a few steelhead and coho.

42 MOSS LAKE

Moss Lake is near Sasquatch Park on the hill above Deer Lake. Access is from Deer Lake over 3.2 kilometers, or 2 miles, of rough road. This small pond has rainbows to 20 centimeters. A hike is required if the gate near Deer Lake is closed.

43 LOOKOUT LAKE

Lookout Lake is 11 hectares or 27 acres and is 40 kilometers or 24.9 miles north of Harrison Mills. A truck or four-wheel-drive is recommended. The lake has excellent rainbow fishing to 35 centimeters or 14 inches.

44 CAMPBELL LAKE

Campbell Lake is a small pond on Mount Woodside, just south of Harrison Hot Springs. It is accessed by a trail from Harrison Hot Springs or via a logging road 11 kilometers or 6.9 miles west of the intersection of Highways 9 and 7 near Agassiz. A truck is recommended. The lake has small rainbows.

45 WILSON LAKE

Wilson Lake is 47 hectares or 116 acres in area and is located 34 kilometers or 21 miles northwest of Harrison Mills. Access is via the Chehalis Lake logging road to an east spur on the south side of Skwellephil Creek. This lake has good catches of rainbow trout.

46 FLORA LAKE

Flora Lake is 16 hectares or 40 acres in size and has excellent fly fishing for rainbows to 50 centimeters or 20 inches. The lake is reached by a 7 kilometer or 4.4 mile trail from Chilliwack Lake Park. The lake lies 55 kilometers or 34.2 miles southeast of Chilliwack.

47 PIERCE LAKE

This small alpine lake is 35 kilometers or 21.5 miles southeast of Chilliwack. The lake is 18 hectares or 44 acres in area and is reached by the Chilliwack Lake Road and a final hike of 8 kilometers or 5 miles. This lake has excellent fly fishing for rainbows to 20 inches or 50 centimeters.

48 CRESCENT LAKE

Crescent Lake is 23 kilometers or 14.3 miles southeast of Hope. Access is via Highway 3 to a logging road 10 kilometers or 6.2 miles east of Hope. There is a final hike of 3 kilometers or 1.9 miles. A truck is recommended. Access is also by the Silver Skagit Road and a very steep climb. Crescent Lake has excellent fly fishing for rainbows to 16 inches or 40 centimeters.

49 HANGING LAKE

Hanging Lake is located on the Canada-United States border 65 kilometers or 40.4 miles southeast of Chilliwack. Access is via the Chilliwack Lake Road, with a final hike of 4 kilometers or 2.5 miles. The lake is 25 hectares or 62 acres in size and was stocked with rainbow trout in the early 1980s. Who knows, by now there may well be 20-inch trout just waiting to be caught! This is another lake for the dedicated, skilled and fit.

IV GAME FISH AND THEIR HABITS

"Fish are still mysterious creatures..."
—Roderick Haig Brown
Fisherman's Fall

THE LIFE CYCLE OF PACIFIC SALMONIDS

There are seven species of Pacific salmonids—five salmon and two trout. The five species of salmon are sockeye, chum, pink, chinook and coho. Only the latter two species—chinook and coho—are sport fish, though chinook has many restrictions in fresh water. The two species of trout are cutthroat and steelhead, both of which are important game fish.

As sexually mature adults, the seven species of salmonids return to their birth stream to spawn. Within days of spawning the five species of salmon die, while cutthroat and steelhead trout may return to saltwater and live to spawn again.

Female salmonids deposit between 2,000 and 4,500 orange red eggs in gravel nests or reeds scooped out of the stream bottom. A large number of eggs is essential, since many biological and environmental factors affect egg survival. Ducks, freshwater fish and a bird known as a dipper eat salmonid eggs during and after the fish have spawned.

Besides natural predators, eggs are sensitive to mechanical shock and bruising for about four weeks after fertilization. Construction projects, clear-cut logging and agriculture all contribute to floods and soil erosion, thus choking off the oxygen supply necessary for egg development.

After salmonids have hatched as alevins, they remain buried under the gravel until their yellow yolk sacs are almost completely absorbed. From the thousands of eggs deposited by a single female, approximately 10 to 15 percent of them hatch to produce alevins that emerge as salmon fry. They have numerous enemies, including freshwater fish, birds, garter snakes, mink and otter. In addition, high water temperature and pollution also affect fry survival.

Depending on species and hazards, only 10 to 30 percent of salmon fry survive to smolt stage. Sockeye females, for example, deposit about 3,000 eggs.

Of these, 450 will emerge as fry and swim to a nearby lake. Of this number, only about 100 smolts will survive to migrate downstream.

After a rearing period in freshwater, smolts undergo physiological changes and are ready to go downstream to the river estuaries. These estuaries are crucial to salmonids, since the smolts feed on insects and crustaceans before migrating out to sea.

Roughly 10 percent or less of smolts survive to adults. Returning to the sockeye example, only six fish of some 100 smolts produced per spawning female reach sexual maturity as adults. Of the six adults, four are caught in ocean fisheries, leaving two remaining adults to migrate to the river mouth. Along the way, sea lions and seals prey on the remaining fish. Freshwater fishermen and the native food fishery take substantial numbers of fish, further reducing their numbers.

Many factors can damage spawning streams including urban development, construction projects and discharge of pollutants. If the spawning area is destroyed the returning adults may seek other areas to spawn or they may die without spawning. If a salmonid dies without spawning, its life cycle in that stream has been broken.

It should be obvious by now that the life cycle of salmonids is difficult and dangerous. Only the fittest and luckiest live to survive as adults and spawn. In areas with good freshwater habitat, salmonid stocks tend to remain stable. Evolution has ensured that salmonid species will survive in spite of natural hazards. However, today human hazards are the greatest threat to salmonids.

SALMONID MIGRATION

Did you ever wonder how salmonids were able to return to their birth stream to spawn? About a year ago, I inquired about salmonid migration to the Federal Fisheries branch in Vancouver. It seems that salmonids use a variety of orientation cues, ranging from gravity, current, odor, landmarks and celestial cues to the earth's magnetic field, the sun and polarized light. The table below indicates the latest scientific thinking about salmonid migration. While this table is for sockeye, it is still relevant for other salmonid species.

Chinook Salmon
Oncorhynchus tshawytscha

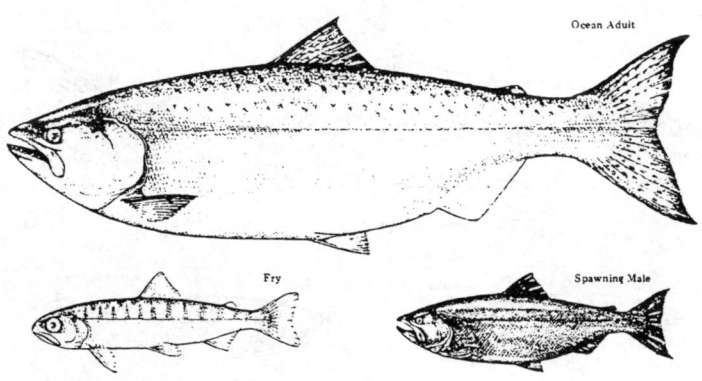

Ocean Adult

Fry

Spawning Male

Coho Salmon
Oncorhynchus kisutch

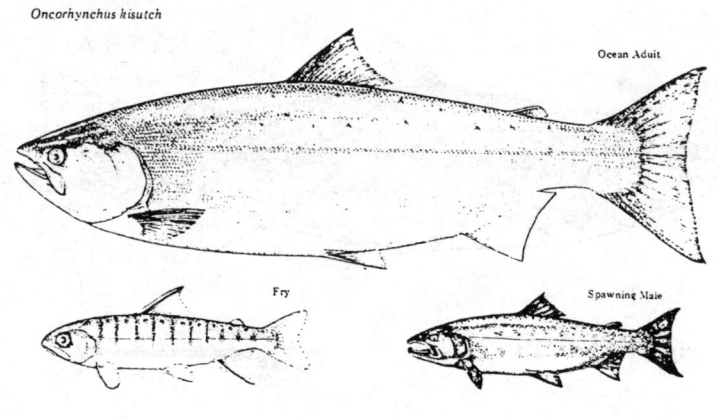

Ocean Adult

Fry

Spawning Male

Cutthroat Trout
Salmo clarki

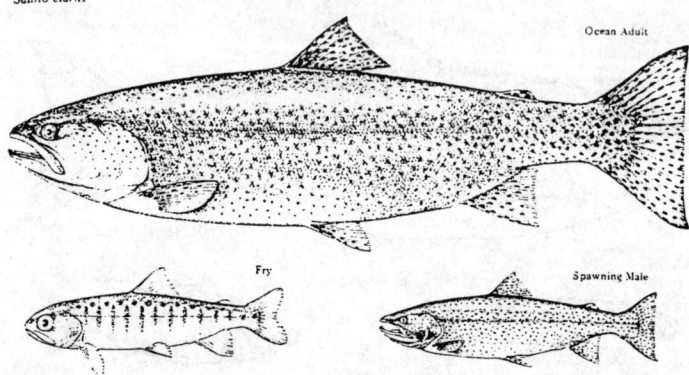

Ocean Adult

Fry

Spawning Male

Steelhead Trout
Salmo gairdneri

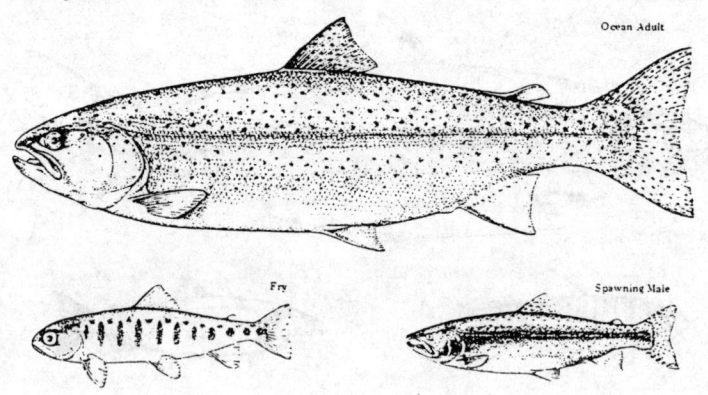

Ocean Adult

Fry

Spawning Male

Table 1

A summary of the orientation cues and orientation mode which sockeye could potentially use during the different habitat changes they perform during a life cycle.

Habitat change	Life stage	Cue
1. Eggs to gravel	alevin	gravity
2. Gravel to river	fry	gravity, current
3. River to lake	fry/fingerlings	current, odor, landmarks, celestial, earth's magnetic field
4. Lake nursery to mouth outlet stream	smolt	sun, polarized light, earth's magnetic field
Mouth outlet stream to estuary		current
5. Estuary to winter grounds	immature	electric potential? celestial? earth's magnetic field?
6-7. Ocean migration	immature	electric potential? celestial, earth's magnetic field?
8. Ocean winter ground to estuary home river	maturing adult	odor/pheromone
9. Estuary to lake outlet	maturing adult	current, odor/pheromone
10. Lake outlet to mouth spawning ground	mature adult	exploratory, celestial? earth's magnetic field?
11. Mouth spawning stream to spawning grounds	mature adult	odor, current

GAME FISH IN THE UPPER FRASER VALLEY

1 CHINOOK

Chinook or springs as they are called in British Columbia, are found in the major streams of the province, especially the Fraser system. After hatching, chinook remain in fresh water from three months to one year. In the ocean, most Canadian chinook remain within 160 kilometers or 100 miles of the Gulf of Alaska.

Chinook adults return to spawn in two to seven years. The two-year fish are the smaller "jacks." These fish are capable of fertilizing eggs which seems to be nature's way of insurance. The four or five year olds are most abundant in southern streams while the six or seven year olds are most abundant in northern streams. Many rivers have two or more stocks of chinook.

Chinook salmon vary between 2 to 14 kilos or 5 to 30 pounds though larger fish are also common. The world record chinook is 57.27 kilograms or 126 pounds.

2 COHO

Coho spawn in over half the 1,500 streams in British Columbia. Young coho spend one or two years in fresh water before migrating as smolts to the ocean, where they spend up to eighteen months before returning to their birth stream to spawn.

Coho enter the sea between April and July each year. Coho from British Columbia move northward, then southward, usually remaining within 40 kilometers or 25 miles of the coast. In late fall and winter, they move south. In spring, the mature coho again migrate northwards until they disperse and return to their birth stream to spawn.

At full growth, coho are from 2.7 to 5.4 kilos or 4 to 12 pounds and grow up to 98 centimeters or 38 inches long. Both coho and chinook have a black mouth, while pinks, chum and sockeye do not. Chinook have black gums while coho have white gums. This should help the novice angler identify chinook and coho salmon.

3 CUTTHROAT TROUT

Coastal or sea-run cutthroat trout spawn in small streams, often close to cities and towns. At full growth, these trout range in weight from 1/4 to 7.8 kilos or 1/2 to 17 pounds. The average size is 45 centimeters or 18 inches long.

Coastal cutthroat usually spawn from February to May depending on water conditions. The young remain in fresh water from one to five years before migrating to the ocean. They usually stay within the estuaries. However, they may stray as much as 16 kilometers or 10 miles from their home estuary. Coastal cutthroat usually spawn for the first time at three or four years and seldom spawn more than twice.

Sea-run cutthroat are beautiful fish, especially when just in from the ocean. With their silvery colored sheen, black speckles and red slash under the jaw, they are truly magnificent.

In southwestern British Columbia, the cutthroat population has recently suffered a decline compared with previous years. This is why all wild cutthroat trout caught in the streams and sloughs of the Upper Fraser Valley must be released. Only hatchery cutthroat can be kept. The difference between a hatchery and a wild fish is that the hatchery fish have their adipose fin missing while wild fish retain their adipose fin. The adipose fin is the small fin on the back near the tail. Please carefully release all wild cutthroat trout caught in streams and sloughs mentioned in this book. Our future fishery depends on healthy stocks of wild fish.

4 STEELHEAD TROUT

Steelhead are sea-going rainbow trout. They are found throughout the coastal rivers of British Columbia. Young steelhead live from one to three years in freshwater before going to the ocean in the spring as smolt. Usually two or more years are spent in the ocean before the fish return to spawn at four or five years of age. After spawning many adult steelhead return to the ocean and between 30 and 60 percent return to fresh water to spawn a second time.

Steelhead spawn in late winter or early spring. They may arrive in fresh water months ahead of spawning or just in time to deposit their eggs. The timing of steelhead runs usually follows an established pattern, year after year. There are sometimes winter, spring and summer runs. Steelhead that return in the summer do not spawn until the following spring.

Steelhead trout are highly prized by anglers because of their fighting abilities. They are perhaps the strongest fish per pound in the world. Mature steelhead usually weigh 3.5 to 4.1 kilos or 8 or 9 pounds, while some may reach 16 kilos or 36 pounds.

5 RAINBOW TROUT

Rainbow trout are nonseagoing cousins of steelhead trout. They are most common in lakes but they enter streams to spawn. The young may spend up to a year in the streams before returning to the lake to grow and mature. Rainbows are second only to steelhead in fighting ability. They tend to strike quickly, jumping numerous times before being landed. Rainbows range from the small 20 centimeter fish found in alpine lakes to the giant 25 kilogram fish taken from Jewel Lake in the Kootenays. These trout readily take a fly, which is perhaps the best way to catch them.

6 DOLLY VARDEN

Dolly Varden are not actually trout; they are char, related to the eastern brook trout and lake trout. Some Dolly Varden spend their entire lives in fresh water while others migrate to the ocean. These fish were once abundant along the Pacific Coast but a combination of habitat destruction and a pernicious bounty reduced their numbers. They are a brightly colored fish, with pink, blue, and yellowish white splotches. The Harrison River and Lake are perhaps the best places to fish for Dolly Varden in this area. These fish readily take bait or lures.

7 KOKANEE

Kokanee are landlocked sockeye salmon spending all their lives in fresh water. Also known as "silver trout," the kokanee usually spawns in its third or fourth year and, like other salmon, dies after spawning. These fish are usually small but may reach 3 pounds or more. The kokanee has deep red flesh which is delicious smoked or cooked. Kawkawa Lake and Jones Lake are the best places to fish for kokanee in this area.

8 WHITEFISH

Whitefish are common in the Lower Fraser system yet these fish are underrated by sportfishermen. These fish look a little like a chub—they have the same sucker mouth—but are whiter with larger scales. Sometimes these fish can surprise you with a strong fight. Be sure to use a small hook.

9 STURGEON

Sturgeon are ancient relics from 300 million years ago. They are found scattered throughout the Lower Fraser system, including Harrison Lake. These fish can weigh several hundred kilos, though you cannot keep the larger specimens. The legal limit for sturgeon is between 100 and 150 centimeters. Smaller and larger fish must be released. You will also need a special sturgeon licence and the yearly quota is only one fish. If you try for sturgeon, be sure to use a hefty rod, sturdy reel and at least 50 pound test line.

10 CARP

In Europe, carp are considered an important game fish; here in Canada they are considered a nuisance. Yet, I have caught carp in Maria Slough that rivalled coho in fighting ability. Carp are a really fine game fish. Use a small hook, light leader, thin float and kernel corn, bread dough or worms for bait. Carp are very light biters so set the hook at the least movement of the float. Carp are best fished in the spring and summer months.

11 NONGAME SPECIES

There are several species of coarse fish, ranging from the small bullhead (a real nuisance) to the larger sucker and squawfish. Chub are also plentiful in the summer months. These fish are found mostly in the Fraser system and not in the numerous lakes, unless they are connected to the Fraser River. While these fish are not prized by anglers, they can still provide much excitement and pleasure, especially for the beginner. Even coarse fish have their place in the fisherman's ethos.

TROUT SHOWING ADIPOSE FIN

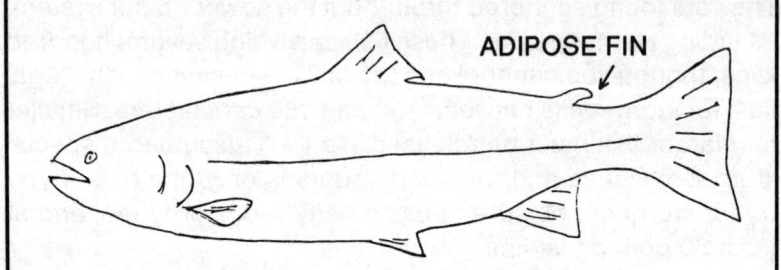

ADIPOSE FIN

TROUT SHOWING CLIPPED ADIPOSE FIN

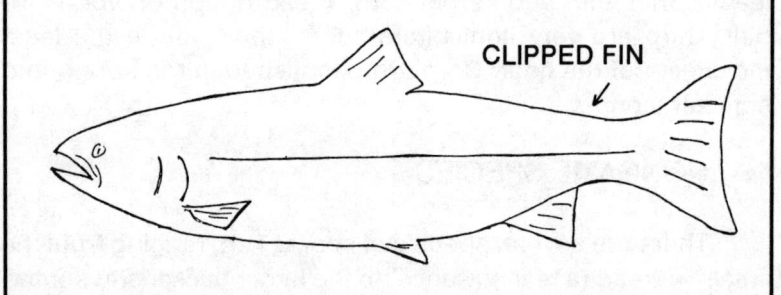

CLIPPED FIN

FISHING TIPS

1) Lighter line gives longer casts and more natural lure action.
2) In midsummer, try fishing in white water and riffles in streams; these oxygenated places are where the trout will be.
3) For best results, fish during the solunar periods and fish early and late. Early and late in the season and early and late in the day.
4) Keep your line tight and rod tip up when handling a fish.
5) In lakes, troll along drop-offs. Bays, points, and boulder strewn bottoms are also good spots. If fishing with a partner, try different lures or flies at different depths.
6) In stream fishing, if you had a fish and lost it leave the pool for an hour or a day. Or switch lures or flies.
7) When fishing lakes, look for midlake shallows. This is a hot spot for fish.
8) If you are breaking off fish, it could be poor handling techniques, brittle line or inadequate line strength, or a rod that is too hefty for the job. Many fish are lost in these ways.
9) Fish are not evenly distributed in lakes and streams. They are often in deeper holes or weedy areas or on boulder strewn bottoms.
10) When releasing fish, be sure to dip your hands in water. Otherwise the sweat and dirt from your hands will remove the mucus from the fish's body, leaving it vulnerable to fungus disease.
11) For best results, fish a stream or lake regularly. This is how 10 percent of fishermen catch 90 percent of all the fish. Familiarity—that's the secret!
12) Location plus timing plus knowledge equals fish. This simple formula is what separates the 10 percent club from the less successful anglers. Knowledge of your fish, the right location and proper timing—that's the winning formula for consistently catching fish.

TACKLE TIPS FOR BEGINNERS

If you are a beginning fisherman and don't quite know what tackle to buy then this section might interest you.

For trout and salmon to 10 pounds, a 6-foot graphite rod will be more than sufficient. These rods are very flexible and absorb the strike of a very large fish. Graphite rods are so flexible that they register even the tiniest of nibbles. As for reels, I suggest an open-spooled reel of medium size. The closed-spooled reels can be frustrating for beginners if the line twists and curls in the spool. As for hooks, size 6 will be sufficient for trout with perhaps a larger hook for salmon. Use these with 8 or 10 pound test line.

If fishing with lures, for this area I recommend bacon and egg, crocodile and coho lures for salmon, while various small spinners and smaller crocodile lures work well for trout. If these fail, try a wedding band lure and worm.

Fly fishing is a delicate art requiring many years of practice to master. It requires knowledge about tackle, flies and fish and insect habitat. Read all you can before committing yourself to buying tackle.

Many people enjoy bait fishing. Some people use leaders off the main fishing line, with the weight at the bottom, while others simply put the hook at the end of the line, with perhaps a small weight 2 or 3 feet from the hook and worm. If fishing with a float and roe, worm or yarn, use about 3 to 6 feet of leader and some weight 2 or 3 feet above the hook. Worms, roe or yarn can be purchased at any of the sports stores mentioned in this book.

If you want to go after really large spring salmon and steelhead trout, I suggest an 8- to 11-foot rod with a heavy reel. Most sportfishermen driftfish for salmon and steelhead so you would have to become familiar with floats, roe and yarn. If using yarn, simply tie or thread a 1-inch piece onto your hook. Be sure to use a larger, sturdier hook for springs and steelhead, with at least 12 pound test line.

For sturgeon fishing, I suggest a large sturdy rod and a heavy reel. Use a large hook threaded with three or four worms. A fishing guide knows the spots where the sturgeon feed.

RELEASING FISH

Catch and release is probably the future for sportfishing in southwestern British Columbia. By following a few simple rules, you can ensure that fish live to spawn or get caught again. Remember that a fish that appears unharmed when released may not survive if carelessly handled.

1) **USE BARBLESS HOOKS**
   Barbless hooks are much easier to remove from the fish's mouth than barbed hooks. A reasonably skilled angler will lose few fish because of barbless hooks.

2) **KEEP YOUR HANDS WET**
   Always wet your hands before touching a fish. Otherwise, dirt and sweat from your hands will remove mucus on the fish, leaving it vulnerable to fungus disease.

3) **TIME IS CRUCIAL**
   Play and release fish as quickly as possible. A fish played too gently for too long may not recover.

4) **KEEP FISH IN WATER AS MUCH AS POSSIBLE**
   A fish out of water is suffocating and may seriously injure itself if allowed to flop on the beach or rocks. Even a few centimeters of water under a thrashing fish acts as a protective buffer.

5) **GENTLENESS IN HANDLING IS NEEDED**
   Keep your fingers out of the gills. Do not squeeze small fish—they are easily held by the lower lip. Try not to entangle the fish's gills in any net you use.

6) **UNHOOKING**
   Remove the hook as rapidly as possible. If the fish is deeply hooked, cut the leader and leave the hook in—do not tear the hook out!

7) **RECOVERING**
   If the fish appears unconscious, always hold the fish in the water (heading upstream in rivers) and propel it back and forth, pumping water through its gills. When the fish is fully recovered let it go to swim away and be caught another day.

SOLUNAR PERIODS

Solunar periods are the times when fish (and game) are actively feeding. These periods were discovered in the nineteenth century by fishermen and hunters. Later they were tabulated, showing the best times to fish or hunt. Solunar periods are associated with the sun, moon, temperature and barometric pressure. Major solunar periods extend from 2 to 3.5 hours while minor periods last about 1 hour.

The most important factor in fishing is barometric pressure. For best results, fish on a rising barometer. A falling barometer seldom produces good catches. Temperature is also an important factor; when the water is too cold or too warm fish are inactive. Temperature ranges between 60 and 68 degrees Fahrenheit are the best for fresh water fishing. Air temperature which is lower than water temperature seldom produces good fishing.

I kept track of the solunar periods in my notes, correlating them with the fish I caught. In a three year period from 1985 to 1987, I found a correlation of 70 percent for the solunar periods. That is, 70 percent of the time I caught fish was associated with a solunar period. This is a significant correlation, enough to make me take solunar periods seriously. For more information about solunar periods and tables, contact Hoshi Enterprises, 753 Kinnear Avenue, Kelowna, B.C., V1Y 5B2.

FISHING LICENSES

For beginners or visitors from other provinces or other countries, fishing licenses are available from the following stores:
1. Rudi's Sports, 7236 Pioneer Avenue, Agassiz
2. Fred's Custom Tackle, 5616 Vedder Road, Vedder Crossing
3. Gord's Tackle, 7300 Vedder Road, Sardis
4. Cheam Sports and Recreation Ltd., 46170 Yale Road, Chilliwack
5. Cheyenne Sports Ltd., 267 Wallace Street, Hope

FISHING GUIDE

For a reliable fishing guide contact:
Cascade Fishing Charters, Comp. 9, Morrow Road, Route 2, Agassiz, B.C. V0M 1A0 phone (604) 796-2125
Fred Helmer, 5616 Vedder Road, Vedder Crossing, B.C. V0X 1Z0 phone (604) 858-7344

STOCKING DATA FOR 1990-1991

	Lake or stream	Date of release	Number	Mean weight grams
1	Coastal Cutthroat (sea-runs)			
	Elbow Lake	91-05-23	2,348	1.3
	Hope River	90-05-09	9,750	66.7
	Maria Slough	91-05-09	3,040	52.6
2	Coastal Cutthroat (nonsea-runs)			
	Deer Lake	90-09-10	9,000	16.2
		91-04-09	8,984	32.6
	Hicks Lake	90-03-27	10,000	31.7
		91-03-12	10,000	27.0
3	Rainbow Trout			
	Elbow Lake	90-05-24	2,000	12.6
	Foley Lake	90-05-19	1,500	172.4
		91-05-07	2,000	12.6
	Francis Lake	90-07-11	500	29.4
		91-06-14	500	21.3
	Grace Lake	90-07-11	1,500	29.4
		91-06-12	1,500	20.0
	Lookout Lake	90-07-11	500	29.4
		91-06-11	500	24.8
	Moss Lake	90-06-12	1,000	15.6
	Weaver Lake	90-04-19	6,000	16.4
		91-06-12	6,300	20.0
4.	Steelhead			
	Coquihala River	90-07-18	86,207	1.6

Note: 454 grams equal 1 pound
Note: Lakes not mentioned are stocked periodically

REFERENCES

Brown, Roderick Haig. *A Primer of Fly Fishing* (New York: William Morrow and Company, 1964).
―――― *Fisherman's Fall* (Toronto: William Colin Sons and Company, 1964).
British Columbia Freshwater Fishing Regulations 1990-1992, available at any tackle shop.
Forest Service Recreational Site Maps—North Fraser Valley, —Chilliwack-Hope, 9850 McGrath, Rosedale, B.C. V0X 1X0.
Groot, Dr. G. *Modification on a Theme—A Perspective on Migratory Behavior of Pacific Salmon* Department of Fisheries and Oceans, Resource Service Branch, Biological Station, Nanaimo, B.C.
Holland, Dan. *The Trout Fisherman's Bible* (Garden City, NY: Doubleday and Company Inc., 1962).
Hoshizaki, Bill ed. *Okay Anglers Fishing Directory* 1984 edition, Hoshi Enterprises, Kelowna, B.C.
Lower Mainland Fishing Guide, B.C. Government, Ministry of Environment 1988 edition, Island Directories, Sidney, B.C.
Lyons, Nick. *The Seasonable Angler* (New York: Simon and Schuster Inc., 1988).
Probert, Richard E. *Fishing Notes.* vol. 1 1983-1986
―――― *Fishing Notes.* vol. 2 1986-1987
―――― *Fishing Notes.* vol. 3 1988-1989
―――― *Fishing Notes.* vol. 4 1990-1991
Release Records Database, Fraser Valley Hatchery, Abbotsford, B.C.

Special thanks go to my numerous fishing contacts, especially to Phil and Carol Boorman.

NOTES:

NOTES:

NOTES:

NOTES:

NOTES:

MORE GREAT HANCOCK HOUSE TITLES

Northern Biographies

Alaska Calls
Virginia Neely
ISBN 0-88839-970-7

Bootlegger's Lady
Sager & Frye
ISBN 0-88839-976-6

Bush Flying
Robert Grant
ISBN 0-88839-350-4

Crazy Cooks and Gold Miners
Joyce Yardley
ISBN 0-88839-294-X

Descent into Madness
Vernon Frolick
ISBN 0-88839-300-8

Fogswamp: Life with Swans
Turner & McVeigh
ISBN 0-88839-104-8

Gang Ranch: Real Story
Judy Alsager
ISBN 0-88839-275-3

Journal of Country Lawyer
Ted Burton
ISBN 0-88839-364-4

Lady Rancher
Gertrude Roger
ISBN 0-88839-099-8

Nahanni
Dick Turner
ISBN 0-88839-028-9

Northern Man
Jim Martin
ISBN 0-88839-979-0

Novice in the North
Bill Robinson
ISBN 0-88839-977-4

Puffin Cove
Neil G. Carey
ISBN 0-88839-216-8

Ralph Edwards of Lonesome Lake
Ed Gould
ISBN 0-88839-100-5

Ruffles on my Longjohns
Isabel Edwards
ISBN 0-88839-102-1

Where Mountains Touch Heaven
Ena Kingsnorth Powell
ISBN 0-88839-365-2

Wings of the North
Dick Turner
ISBN 0-88839-060-2

Yukon Lady
Hugh McLean
ISBN 0-88839-186-2

Yukoners
Harry Gordon-Cooper
ISBN 0-88839-232-X

Outdoor Titles

12 Basic Skills of Flyfishing
Ted Peck & Ed Rychkun
ISBN 0-88839-392-X

Adventure with Eagles
David Hancock
ISBN 0-88839-217-6

Alpine Wildflowers
Ted Underhill
ISBN 0-88839-975-8

Birds of North America
David Hancock
ISBN 0-88839-220-6

Coastal Lowland Flowers
Ted Underhill
ISBN 0-88839-973-1

Eastern Rocks & Minerals
James Grandy
ISBN 0-88839-105-6

Eastern Mushrooms
Barrie Kavasch
ISBN 0-88839-091-2

Edible Seashore
Rick Harbo
ISBN 0-88839-199-4

Guide to Collecting Wild Herbs
Julie Gomez
ISBN 0-88839-390-3

Northeastern Wild Edibles
Barrie Kavasch
ISBN 0-88839-090-4

Orchids of North America
Dr. William Petrie
ISBN 0-88839-089-0

Pacific Wilderness
Hancock, Hancock & Sterling
ISBN 0-919654-08-8

Roadside Wildflowers NW
Ted Underhill
ISBN 0-88839-108-0

Sagebrush Wildflowers
Ted Underhill
ISBN 0-88839-171-4

Seashells of the Northeast Coast
Gordon & Weeks
ISBN 0-88839-808-7

Tidepool & Reef
Rick Harbo
ISBN 0-88839-039-4

Trees of the West
Mabel Crittenden
ISBN 0-88839-269-9

Upland Field and Forest Wildflowers
Ted Underhill
ISBN 0-88839-171-4

Western Mushrooms
Ted Underhill
ISBN 0-88839-031-9

Wildflowers of the West
Mabel Crittenden
ISBN 0-88839-270-2

Wild Harvest
Terry Domico
ISBN 0-88839-022-X

Wildlife of the Rockies
Hancock & Hall
ISBN 0-919654-33-9

Native Titles

Ah Mo
Tren J. Griffin
ISBN 0-88839-244-3

American Indian Pottery
Sharon Wirt
ISBN 0-88839-134-X

Argillite
Drew & Wilson
ISBN 0-88839-037-8

Art of the Totem
Marius Barbeau
ISBN 0-88839-168-4

Coast Salish
Reg Ashwell
ISBN 0-88839-009-2

End of Custer
Dale Schoenberger
ISBN 0-88839-288-5

Haida: Their Art and Culture
Leslie Drew
ISBN 0-88839-132-3

Hunters of the Buffalo
R. Stephen Irwin
ISBN 0-88839-176-5

Hunters of the Forest
R. Stephen Irwin
ISBN 0-88839-175-7

MORE GREAT HANCOCK HOUSE TITLES

Rafe Mair
ISBN 0-88839-346-6
5 1/2 X 8 1/2, 160 pp.

Barry Thornton
ISBN 0-88839-370-9
5 1/2 X 8 1/2, 192 pp.

Barry Thornton
ISBN 0-88839-268-0
5 1/2 X 8 1/2, 168 pp.

David Nuttall
ISBN 0-88839-097-1
5 1/2 X 8 1/2, 184 pp.

Ed Rychkun
ISBN 0-88839-338-5
5 1/2 X 8 1/2, 120 pp.

Ed Rychkun
ISBN 0-88839-305-9
5 1/2 X 8 1/2, 96 pp.

Eric Carlisle
ISBN 0-88839-212-5
5 1/2 X 8 1/2, 192 pp.

Ed Rychkun
ISBN 0-88839-339-3
5 1/2 X 8 1/2, 238 pp.

Ed Rychkun
ISBN 0-88839-377-6
5 1/2 X 8 1/2, 272 pp.

Available from Hancock House Publishers 19313 Zero Ave., Surrey, B.C. V4P 1M7
1-800-938-1114 Credit cards accepted. 1431 Harrison Ave., Blaine, WA 98230